Contents

Introduction

The business of being a corporate home economist is busy, vibrant and really a little boutique. The industry is made up of mostly women (but there are a couple of dedicated males thrown in). It's a career not really known by many and often questioned, with people often asking 'What is it you actually do?'

I was always destined to be involved with food. The decision to be formally trained and skilled in recipe creation, food writing, food styling, presenting or formal teaching was so the right one for me … it had me in its grips immediately.

On completing the necessary training at East Sydney Technical College, I was thrust into a marvellous world of test kitchens. I have been so lucky to work within test kitchens, and film and food studios as a freelance home economist.

Cooking and a love of food cooked well is finally 'all the rage' again. Thank goodness! But so many of the tried and true, gospel techniques have vanished. These little tips and tricks that were once handed down from mother to daughter or family-to-family are now 'secrets'.

Our televisions are filled with wonderful, inspirational, often gourmet standard, recipes, but the day-to-day basics— well, it is presumed everyone knows them. I must confess I am a real 'sensible pants'. This has greatly assisted me in my career, as I look for the commonsense approach. I thrive on the whole experience of purchasing fabulous food. It could be at local farmers markets, big bustling fresh food markets or small local providers. I love chatting with growers, merchants, butchers, the egg lady, the honey man and the herb man. Wandering into a market and seeing the abundance of beautiful fresh produce, experiencing the seasons through food and the many varieties is such joy. As a busy working mother I truly understand the pressure of having to shop, cook and get it all done. Supermarkets are a convenience. If you are a regular supermarket goer, do yourself a favour, sift through and demand the quality you want from your supermarket. It is there, so always ask questions, smell, sniff and taste.

As a wife and mother of teenagers it helps that I understand what it's like in a busy household. I get the demands of the everyday life and the seemingly impossible task of eating well, not wasting food and, most importantly, loving every mouthful of what you cook. Incorporating a busy work and family life is a challenge and to add to it all there are some food intolerences. For the most part, much of my diet is gluten free. Although I am not a true coeliac, I just feel better when I limit the amount of wheat I eat. I also enjoy using other flours that are gluten-free. This is not a gluten-free cookbook, but I have added some recipes and chatted about some of the other flours to use. For the real information, I so strongly recommend Dr Sue Shepherd, who has written several fabulous cookbooks. So grab a cup of tea or maybe a glass of wine and sit back, relax and read through a food skills guide. I hope you enjoy reading some of the secrets I have learnt over the years.

Jo

THE SIX THINGS I CAN'T LIVE WITHOUT

My KitchenAid® standmixer

Good-quality chicken (free-range at least)

The best eggs I can find (I love organic!)

Salt flakes

Good quality unsalted butter

Vegetables (fresh and seasonal!)

Of course, there is so much more but one has
to draw the line somewhere!

THE BASICS

What's needed in the kitchen

- Standmixer, good quality
- Food processor, good quality
- Chopping boards, large and strong: preferably a selection (one for meats, one for chicken, one for fruit and vegetables)
- Knives: The minimum is one cook's knife (around 7¾in/20cm), one large serrated knife, one paring/small knife
- Stainless steel saucepans: (with tight-fitting lids and ovenproof handles!) 1 x 14¾ pints (7 litre) (optional but good big size for loads of soup, pasta etc), 1 x 8½ pints (4 litre), 2 x 4 pints (2 litre), 1 x 2 pints (1 litre)
- Frying pans/wok: 1 large 9½in (24cm) good quality non-stick, 1 smaller, around 7¾in (20cm),1 medium-sized carbon steel wok and a lid is needed! (Remember to note if your cooktop is gas or electric; electric needs a flat bottom wok)
- Baking dishes: 1 large (for something like a roast), 1 smaller square or round (for something like a scalloped potatoes)
- Lasagna dish: not only for lasagna, but also good for roasting and baking and serving
- Cake pans: (your choice of PushPan or classic style) 2 x 7¾in (20cm) round, 1 x 8½in (22cm) round, 1 x 7¾in (20cm) square, 1 x loaf pan, 1 x 6-hole ½ cup muffin/cupcake pan
- Baking sheets: 2 x non-stick flat trays with a small lip, 1 x slice pan (approximately 6⅓ x 10⅓in/16 x 26cm)
- Cooling racks (you will need two!)
- Scales (preferably electronic!)
- Kitchen timer
- Measuring cups and measuring spoons (metric measurements have been used here—be careful here as all countries have different sizes and capacities—see International Terms page 28).
- Mixing bowls: selection of various sizes from large to very small
- Colander
- Sieve (fine)
- Culinary tools: silicon spatulas x 2, wooden spoon, large metal spoon, slotted spoon, can opener, kitchen scissors, small balloon whisk, pastry brush, tongs x 2 (metal with silicon tipped and long handles), ladle, fine hand-grater, large 'box' grater, citrus juicer.

What's needed in the pantry

Spices

There are so many to use and choose but I can't live without:

Ground cumin

Ground coriander

Ground cinnamon

Chilli flakes

Curry powder

Ground nutmeg

Paprika (sweet and smoked)

Peppercorns (whole black)

Herbs

(preferably fresh)

Bay leaves (dried are OK)

Coriander/cilantro

Chives

Basil

Thyme

Oregano

Oils

Extra virgin olive oil

Pure olive oil

Sunflower oil

Sesame oil

Baking

Baking powder

Coconut (desiccated and shredded)

Vanilla extract

Almond meal

Hazelnut meal

Almonds, blanched, slivered

Walnuts (good quality)

Flours

Plain (all-purpose) flour (wheat)

Self-raising flour (wheat)

Plain (gluten-free flour)

Cornflour (cornstarch) (maize)

Potato flour

Fine rice flour (white)

Sugar

Caster (superfine)

Brown

Rice

Jasmine

Basmati

Arborio

Sauces, Vinegars, Pastes and Stocks

Sea salt flakes

Cooking salt

Tomato paste

Green/red curry paste

Sweet chilli sauce

Soy sauce

Balsamic vinegar

White wine vinegar

Prepared chicken, vegetable or beef stock in liquid, concentrated or dried powder/ cube form

If choosing gluten-free, read the labels carefully.

A BIT ABOUT HERBS

Fresh, fresh, fresh is best, best, best! But ... dried herbs do have a place. Some herbs, such as basil, are not always available, especially in the cooler months. Generally speaking, use about one-third to one-half of the dried to the fresh amount. If the dried herbs are recently dried, they will have more flavour.

Storage

The best way is to grow your own fresh herbs, snip them and rinse them (lightly pat with paper afterwards) before using. But I do understand this is just not always possible so yes buy fresh! But once you buy fresh how do you keep them fresh? I like herbs to last for at least five days and this truly is possible if you follow these little tips.

1. If the bunch has roots—leave them! I love to use the crushed or finely chopped roots in curry pastes and stirfries (cook them with other aromatics like garlic and ginger).
2. Refresh the herbs (particularly if a little dehydrated and sad). I fill the sink with cold water and let the bunch (or bunches) 'swim'. Leave them in the cold water for about 20 minutes and you'll be amazed how beautifully they revive.
3. Remove the bunch from the water, gently shake off the excess water. Now lightly roll each bunch in plain paper towel (a couple of times over). This keeps the herbs moist and protected from the harsh drying cold of the fridge.
4. Place the paper towel-wrapped bunch into a flat sealed container or large plastic bag and seal with a little air trapped in. Place in the fridge where the bag won't be squashed!
5. To use, open the bag or container, remove the paper and use as needed. Then rewrap remaining herbs and store as before. If the paper towel has dried out completely, spray or sprinkle with more cold water. Place into the bag, seal and pop back into the fridge.

Tip: The paper needs to be moist, not the herb. If herbs are wet this will encourage slimy spots—yuk!

The herbs you must have

Parsley (curly or flat leaf)

Thyme

Basil

Oregano

Coriander/cilantro

Then: chives, common garden mint, Vietnamese mint, marjoram and the list goes on ...

BAKING KNOW-HOW

The four to-dos before you begin

- weigh and measure
- preheat oven
- position your shelves in the right position
- butter and flour pan, or grease and line with baking paper

Two important extras

- Clean up as you go. A sink filled with hot soapy water is handy, as you can rinse and stack or rinse and pop in the dishwasher as you go.
- READ THE RECIPE completely through at least twice before you begin.

Oven

Buy a small inexpensive oven thermometer from a hardware or cookware store and pop it into the centre of the oven. The dial on your oven is very often nothing like the actual temperature reading! Even 50°F (10°C) can make a difference to your baking.

Oven shelves

I like to move the shelves around as required. Some foods, particularly baked goods, will benefit from being placed in the 'right' section of the oven. Most recipes in this book will advise you where the best position is.

To fan or not to fan

I must confess I am not a fan of the fan, being the fan-forced oven! The old-fashioned way is for me. Really the only time I use the fan is for crackling, some pastries and possibly scones. For me, I think a dry static heat is much better for all types of cooking. If you can't turn your fan off, lower the temperature of the oven by at least 70°F (20°C), lower the shelf (more about this in the next paragraph), and pop an ovenproof shallow container (maybe an old pie plate or cake pan) filled with water into the bottom of the oven. I find the moist air produces a much better result—give it a try!

Positioning of shelves

Most of us were taught to cook right in the centre of the oven. I feel that for some cakes, biscuits and pastries the heat is too direct! I personally like to cook in the lower third of the oven. This positions the top of the cake pan in the centre of the oven. If you have been a little unhappy with your baked results, try this. However, if I am using two shelves in the oven, I rotate the trays or pans half way through the cooking time to ensure an even result.

Get ready

It so helps, in fact it's essential, for you to have all the ingredients weighed and measured BEFORE you begin. I even have it all placed on a tray. Without it all together, I know I will forget to add something. Working from a tray also keeps me a bit more neat and tidy! Well it helps anyway …

Which gluten-free flour?

Gluten strengthens and binds dough in baking. The flours listed below are alternatives to wheat flour and are all wheat- and gluten-free. However, recipes made with wheat-free alternative flours will always be different from those containing wheat.

I mostly like to make it easy for myself when adapting a recipe to gluten-free. So I have found using a premix gluten-free flour with a 'gum' already added suits me best. There are a few brands around and with a little 'experimenting' you will find they work very well.

Most pre-packed gluten-free flours are a combination of three to four flours and normally speaking these are rice, corn, tapioca and/or potato flours. Some are already combined with a gum to add strength and firmness.

I thought it might be good reading to write a little about some of these readily available wheat flour alternatives, so keep reading on.

Arrowroot flour is from the root of the arrowroot plant. A great tasteless thickener! It also becomes clear when cooked, so it's great for thickening sauces.

Buckwheat flour is not actually wheat at all. It has a stronger 'earthy' flavour and is heavier in texture. It's good when used in heavier style cakes and pancakes or pikelets.

Cornflour is a must have for all gluten-free eaters. It is used widely as a thickener or base of many cakes and biscuits. It is normally combined with rice flour in baking. Remember to use maize cornflour (cornstarch) only.

Potato starch (often also called potato flour) is a very fine white powder; it produces a 'lighter' texture in baking than using cornflour. Fabulous for lightly thickening, dusting and good in biscuits and cakes when combined with rice flour.

Rice flour—white (I particularly like the finer Asian-style rice flours). These are very fine in texture and produce a lighter result than Western rice flours. Good as a thickener or base for sauces. It's great for use in biscuits and cakes. Normally combined with other flours to produce a gluten-free flour mixture

Brown rice flour, from unpolished brown rice, still contains the bran. It is therefore higher in fibre and better for you health-wise, but I also find it adds a delicious nutty flavour.

Soy flour is high in protein and fat. It has a strong 'nutty' taste and can have a bitter flavour that is noticeable to many. This bitterness reduces on baking. Some prepacked gluten-free flour mixes have soy flour as it produces a firmer texture. Often found in gluten-free bread mixtures. Best stored in a sealed container in the refrigerator, as it can turn rancid quickly.

Tapioca flour, from the root of a cassava plant, is a great thickener for sauces. It adds a texture and "chewiness" to cakes. It is also good when making gluten free pasta.

Quinoa flour (said 'keen wah'), is an 'older' grain. It has been around for 1000's of years. A versatile flour now very popular because it has good protein content. It bakes well in cakes and breads and slices. Good when combined with rice flour.

Gluten-free adaptations

In this book I have selected some essential recipes that are easily adapted gluten-free eating. To make this as easy as possible I have used a pre-packaged gluten free flour that contains a 'gum'. These are available at supermarkets and if you read the back of the packet it will indicate this. If unsure, talk to someone at your local health food store who will be able to help. However, if you wish to make your own gluten-free flour mix I suggest this as a base.

Combine these four flours for a general homemade all-purpose flour

All-purpose gluten-free flour mix

¼ cup (approx. 35g/1¼oz) cup fine white rice flour

¼ cup (approx. 40g/1½oz) potato starch flour

¼ cup (approx. 35g/1¼oz) maize cornflour (cornstarch)

¼ cup (approx. 30g/1oz) tapioca flour

½ teaspoon xanthan gum (or guar gum)

This will make approximately 1 cup (135g/4½oz gluten-free flour)

Place in a bowl and stir well with a balloon whisk or combine in the food processor.

An additional ½ teaspoon gum may be added if desired for pastry, but go easy as it will dry out the baked product.

For gluten-free self-raising flour: add 2 teaspoons gluten free baking power to every 1 cup (approx. 135g/4½oz) flour mix.

Gluten-free baking is a science, but with a little understanding and a commitment to success you will succeed! I have several recipes in my baking repertoire that many people enjoy and simply do not know or believe are gluten-free.

Remember:

- Always check ingredient labels before cooking gluten-free food, especially sauces and condiments.
- Most gluten-free flours are available in the health food aisle of supermarkets or from health food stores.

Baking recipes

Many recipes in this book can be easily adapted to gluten-free (with a good result), simply by removing the plain flour (all-pupose flour) and replacing with the homemade premix gluten-free flour or a pre-packaged gluten-free flour.

Please be sure to allow the baked cake, biscuit or slice to COOL completely before moving. (Don't touch it!) Gluten-free baked food is softer than standard baked goods. It will firm completely once it has totally cooled. Patience, patience, patience.

The baking recipes that you can easily adapt to be gluten-free are marked with this symbol. GF

Separating eggs

This is really a practice makes perfect thing. Initially go slowly and calmly. Begin with two bowls: gently crack the egg on the edge of a bowl OR use a flat-bladed bread and butter knife and tap it on the side of the egg.

Prise open the two halves over one of the bowls. Let the egg white fall into one of the bowls and gently transfer the yolk back and forth between the two egg-shell halves. Place the egg yolk in the other bowl. If a smidge of yolk falls into the white it must be taken out! You can try very gently using the edge of the shell to scoop out the yolk from the whites!

Measuring: dry ingredients

The best method for dry ingredients is to use scales. Otherwise use measuring cups. But please be aware not all cups are equal! American cup sizes are 8½oz (237g). The British cup size is 10oz (284g). The cup size we have used in this book is metric at 9oz (250g).

Tablespoon measures

The tablespoon measurements used in this book are ⅔oz (20ml/20g). Standard imperial measurements (such as those for USA and UK tablespoons) are ½oz (15g).

This can be a problem with a sauce (something like a white sauce), as you need the correct amount of flour. In baking it really will not matter.

Filling a measuring cup

When adding flour and sugar to a measuring cup, don't 'scoop' it in but add it in with a large spoon. Tap the cup firmly on the bench and level off with a knife.

Measuring: liquid ingredients

Use a liquid measuring jug (not a dry ingredients measuring cup). This can be glass, metal or plastic and have measurement markings on the side.

For best results place the jug on the bench and pour in the liquid. Lean down and look at the measurement, keeping it level, don't lift the cup up to your eye (this method will not be accurate).

Sifting

No, I am not a fan of sifting! It simply seems boring and takes time. There are quicker methods than the conventional method!

Many flours are now presifted before packaging thankfully. If I do need to sift or combine ingredients together I will either pop them into a small bowl and using a little hand balloon whisk, combine them together OR pop the ingredients into my standmixer with the beater or whisk attachments and mix on speed 1 until combined.

Flouring the bench

This is simply dusting the clean dry bench with plain (all-purpose) flour. Don't overdo it, just enough to stop the dough sticking.

To butter, flour and/or line the base and sides

I always butter the base and sides of cake pans and lightly flour or line with baking paper; even non-stick pans. The side texture of your cake is simply better when you do this. The exception to this rule is sponge cakes. DO NOT line the sides of the pan for a sponge, only the base. (see recipe, page 148)

To butter and flour: generously butter the base and sides of the pan with a good smear of butter on a piece of paper towel or if you prefer you can use melted butter with a pastry brush. Then add about 2 tablespoons plain (all-purpose) flour and knock it around the pan to lightly coat the base and sides, then turn the pan upside down and lightly tap it to remove the excess flour.

To line the pan: cut a circle of baking paper by tracing around the outside of the pan. Cut out the paper with a sharp pair of scissors. Measure the height of the sides and cut a thick large strip of baking paper to fit around the inside edge of the pan. Generously butter the base and sides of the pan with butter on a piece of paper towel or if you prefer you can use melted butter and spread it on with a pastry brush. Place the circle of paper in the base and smooth it over. Place the paper around the sides and using your fingertips rub the paper around to secure.

Turning out your cakes

I like to use two cake racks for this. Allow your cooked cake to sit 5–10 minutes (depending on the style of cake) to rest. You normally never turn out a cake straight away.

Spring form pan: Release the spring on the side and lift off the round outside. Turn the cake over onto a cake rack and carefully remove the pans base and baking paper. Sit the second cake rack on top and carefully turn over. Allow to cool completely.

PushPan (pull down outsides): sit the cake on a small stand (something like a can) and firmly pull the sides down to release. Turn the cake over onto a cake rack and remove the pan base and baking paper. Sit the second cake rack onto top and turn the cake over. Allow to cool completely.

Standard cake pan: turn the cake pan over carefully but confidently out onto a cake rack and lift off cake pan. Carefully remove the baking paper. Place the second cake rack on top and carefully flip the cake over. Allow to the cake to cool completely. Placing a tea towel over the cake rack will stop lines from the rack being indented into the cake.

How do I know when it's cooked?

Cakes: all cakes should be firm and golden. The centre of the cake should be firm. Sometimes this is difficult so in some recipes you will see I have advised to cover the cake about half way through the cooking with a large sheet of buttered foil (so the foil won't stick to the cake). The remainder of the cooking is done 'covered' and the cake centre will steam through.

Biscuits: all biscuits will be firm and lightly golden, but still a little soft when in the oven, but will continue to firm on cooling. Let the biscuits stand 5 minutes on the baking tray before moving to a cooling rack.

Blind baking: this is precooking a pastry shell before the filling is added. If you want a crisp base, you must blind bake! To blind bake, place the pastry-lined tart shell onto a baking tray. Place a sheet of baking paper gently on top of the pastry and fill the centre with baking weights, dried beans or rice or even plain (all-purpose) flour. Bake the shell for about 12–15 minutes. Carefully remove the baking paper and weights. Return the pastry shell to the oven for a further 5 minutes. The tart is now ready for the filling. The 'baking' rice and beans can be used over and over. Just remember that once used for blind baking, the rice and beans cannot be cooked and eaten.

Fish

The fish will flake easily when it's gently 'tested' with a tip of a knife. Fish is overcooked by many, not undercooked! The actual cooking time depends on the thickness of the fillet or whole fish. Some fish, such as salmon and tuna, should be eaten a little undercooked and still very pink in the centre.

Potatoes

Potatoes are a vegetable that must be cooked until tender! The tenderness is tested with the piecing of a knife. The knife should go into the potato cleanly. But don't overcook or the potato will fall apart!

Rice

Rice is cooked until it's just tender but not mushy! The grains should be swollen and looking plump but not mushy or waterlogged. Risotto and pilaf are served cooked but a little 'al dente', meaning that the rice has a little bite left in it. Often the rice is cooked until just under and then allowed to stand covered to finish cooking. for 2–3 minutes. Don't worry: the rice will not go cold.

Pastry success: a perfect shell in 16 steps

1. CHILL! Keep it cool! This includes the room (if it's hot, use air conditioning or a fan). Chill the butter and your hands! If your hands are too warm you will 'oil' the butter.
2. Measure the flour accurately (I like to use scales).
3. Follow the recipe, don't OVERmix or process as the pastry will become tough.
4. Make the pastry, form it into a ball and wrap in plastic wrap. Refrigerate for 20 minutes minimum. Pastry can be made up to five days before using.
5. Remove the pastry from the refrigerator (if it's very firm and cold set aside for 10 minutes).
6. How to roll out: dust the bench and the rolling pin very lightly with plain (all-purpose) flour.
7. Start in the centre of the pastry and roll from the centre out—moving around to the next section and repeat, rolling from the centre out, forming a circle shape as you go
8. Don't roll over the pastry edges—this will help make the pastry shrink.
9. Roll out to a circle about 2–3cm (about 1in) larger than the plate/ tin / dish you are lining.

10. If the pastry is getting a little warm (and sweaty and sticky), place it back into the refrigerator for 10 minutes (pastry likes to be kept cool).

11. To move the pastry—gently lift the edge of the pastry over the rolling pin (kind of folding it over the pin). Lift it up and place over the dish or plate.

12. Lay the pastry into the dish, allowing it to fall in.

13. Holes or tears? Patch them with a little pastry from the outside edge.

14. Trim off the excess pastry with a small knife. (Or you can gently roll the rolling pin over the edge of the plate or dish).

15. Blind bake the pastry. Lay a clean sheet of baking paper over the pastry. Fill the cavity with dried beans or rice or baking weights. Bake for 15 minutes in a 400°F (190–200°C) oven (depending on your recipe).

16. Remove the paper and the dried or metal filling and return the pastry shell to the oven. Bake for another 5–8 minutes or until lightly golden and firm.

In this book we used

- Eggs: large 2oz/60g
- Milk: full cream or full fat
- Butter: unsalted for sweet recipes; salted for savoury
- Sugar: caster (superfine)
- Cream: 35% milk fat, thickened or pouring
- Cocoa: unsweetened, preferably best-quality, dark, baking cocoa or Dutch processed
- Chocolate: please choose the best quality couverture chocolate with a good amount of cocoa solids (minimum 70%). If at all possible don't use a 'compound' chocolate—as they can contain many emulsifiers and too much sugar.
- Stock: choose a premade stock made with natural ingredients. Preferably a liquid stock. Salt-reduced is a good choice and many premade stocks are very salty.

International Terms

self-raising flour | self-rising flour	cream (35%) | single cream
plain flour | all-purpose flour	rocket | arugula
cornflour | corn starch	sea salt flakes | kosher salt
caster sugar | granulated or superfine sugar	plastic wrap | cling film
icing sugar | confectioners sugar	baking paper | parchment paper

Oven Temperatures

Fahrenheit	Celcius	Gas mark	Termed
200°F	100°C	--------	very cool
240°F	120°C	--------	cool / low / slow
260°F	130°C	1	cool / low / slow
275°F	140°C	2	slow
300°F	150°C	3	slow
325°F	170°C	4	moderately slow
350°F **	180°C **	5 **	moderate
375°F **	190°C **	6 **	moderate
400°F **	200°C **	7 **	hot
425°F	220°C	8	hot
450°F	230°C	9	very hot

** most commonly used

GENERAL TIPS

Rice

There are many varieties of rice and some are more suited to various styles of cooking than others.

- Basmati: a long grain rice with a lovely texture. Very suited to curries and pilaf.
- Arborio: a short grain rice that produces a delicious starchy result.
- Jasmine: an aromatic long grain rice, perfect with Thai-style recipes
- Basic long grain: a simple, plain rice, neutral flavour.
- Brown rice: nutty flavoured with a firmer texture. It is a healthier choice as it is a good source of fibre.
- Storage: rice is best stored in an airtight container.

Meat

Beef and lamb

- Buy the best you can afford. I always chat with the butcher as to what I am cooking and what's 'good' today and if you have a good butcher, stay with them! You do get what you pay for! Cheap meat? Well, it can taste like cheap meat!
- Red meat should look fresh, clean, firm and have nice white firm fat. Yes, you can trim the fat, but remember it's needed for flavour. Once home remove the meat from the packaging, pat dry with paper towel and place on a paper towel, lined plate. Cover with plastic wrap and refrigerate.

- Beef and lamb are best eaten within two to three days of purchase. Otherwise it's best to freeze. Mince, however, should be eaten as soon as possible. (I always use the mince on the day purchased; often I mince my own.)
- Cuts and cooking: tender cuts are best for quicker cooking methods. Firmer cuts will need long slow cooking at a lower temperature to tenderise. Chat with the butcher as to what you are cooking. Also see the meat cut recommended in the recipe.
- Standing and resting: essential technique if you have cooked a steak or a roast. A very important step that allows the meat to rest giving you a softer more succulent result. Often resting can be around a third of the cooking time.
- Freezing: cover with plastic wrap or place into a bag and seal. Label with cut of meat and date. Freeze for up to three months.
- Defrosting: best done in a clean spot (I like to use a clean kitchen sink). If possible remove the outside covering and place on a plate or rack, this way the juices can drain away. The defrosting time depends on the room temperature. The frozen meat can also be left to defrost in the refrigerator. This takes longer but is a better food safety option in warm weather.
- Meat should have NO smell!

Pork

- Buy the best you can afford.
- There are definitely various qualities of pork. Cheap pork will taste like cheap pork! I like free-range pork and prefer a local, quality product—don't be scared to ask questions about what you're buying like 'where does is come from?'.
- Pork should look 'fresh', clean and be very pale pink with nice-looking, firm, very white fat.
- Once home remove the pork from the packaging, pat dry with paper towel and place on paper towel-lined plate. Cover with plastic wrap and refrigerate.
- Pork is best eaten within one to two days of purchasing. Otherwise it's best to freeze. Mince, however, should be eaten as soon as possible. I always use the mince on the day purchased, often I mince my own.
- Cuts and cooking: pork is a lean meat and care must be taken not to dry it out. Tender cuts are best for quicker cooking methods. Firmer cuts will need long, slow cooking at a lower temperature to tenderise. Chat with the butcher as to what you are cooking. Also see the meat cut recommended in the recipe.
- Standing and resting: essential technique if you have cooked a pork steak, cutlet or a roast. A very important step that allows the meat to rest giving you a softer more succulent result (Often resting can be around a third of the cooking time)
- Freezing: cover with plastic wrap or place into a bag and seal. Label with cut of meat and date. Freeze for up to 3 months.
- Defrosting: best done in a clean spot (I like to use a clean kitchen sink). If possible remove the outside covering and place on a plate or rack, this way the juices can drain away. The defrosting time depends on the room temperature. The frozen pork can also be left to defrost in the refrigerator. This takes longer but is a better food safety option in warm weather. Take care with pork as once defrosted the pork must be refrigerated immediately until use.
- Pork should have NO smell.
- Only buy female pork as it is lighter, more tender and jucier. Check with your butcher!

Chicken

- Buy the best you can afford. Definitely free-range or limited chemical processing. Organic is the best, so if available—buy it.
- Chicken should look 'fresh', clean and be pale pink with nice looking firm whitish skin. The exception to this is corn-fed chicken, it will have a yellow tinge to the flesh and skin.
- Once home remove the chicken from the packaging, pat dry with paper towel and place on a paper towel-lined plate. Cover with plastic wrap and refrigerate.
- Chicken is best eaten within one to two days of purchase. Otherwise it's best to freeze.
- Cuts and cooking: the breast fillet and thigh fillet are interchangeable in recipes, but the breast fillet is lean and easily dries out: so care is needed not to overcook. (I tend to like the texture and flavour of a thigh fillet).
- Standing and resting: standing time is a good technique after char grilling or roasting a whole chicken. The chicken will taste more tender and have a nice succulence (see each recipe for standing time).
- Freezing: cover with plastic wrap or place into a bag and seal. Label with cut of chicken and date. Freeze for up to 3 months.
- Defrosting: best done in a clean spot (I like to use a clean kitchen sink). If possible remove the outside covering and place on a plate or rack, this way the juices can drain away. The defrosting time depends on the room temperature. The frozen chicken can also be left to defrost in the refrigerator. This takes longer but is a better food safety option in warm weather. Take care with chicken as once defrosted the chicken must be refrigerated immediately until use.
- Chicken should have NO smell.

Fish

- Always, always, always buy the freshest you can find. Be aware that if the fish has been frozen you must NOT freeze it again! Fish should look 'fresh', clean and should smell 'fresh from the sea'.
- Once home, remove the fish from the packaging, pat dry with paper towel and place on a paper towel-lined plate. Cover with plastic wrap and refrigerate.
- Fish is best eaten on the day of purchase. Otherwise it's best to freeze.
- Cooking: for all recipes in this book, quick cooking is the best! Remember fish overcooks very quickly.
- Freezing: cover with plastic wrap or place into a bag and seal. Label with cut of fish and date. Freeze for up to three months.
- Defrosting: best done in a clean spot (I like to use a clean kitchen sink). If possible remove the outside covering and place on a plate or rack, this way the juices can drain away). The defrosting time depends on the room temperature. The frozen fish can also be left to defrost in the refrigerator. This takes longer but is a better food safety option in warm weather. Take care with fish as once defrosted the fish must be refrigerated immediately until use.
- Fish should have NO smell, just a pleasant slight ocean aroma.

Eggs

- Always buy the best eggs you can afford. Always buy free-range if not organic.
- Store in the carton in the fridge. The carton helps to keep other odours out (eggs are porous). Don't store out of the fridge—they become stale very quickly.
- Most important tip: always warm (in a bowl of warm water) before boiling, poaching or using in cake mixtures.

Bread

- For best results with all bread recipes, buy a good flavoursome loaf of bread and hand cut the slices! Otherwise choose a heavy firm pre-cut bread. The light sweet thin stuff just doesn't 'cut it'!
- Always buy a natural bread or if possible a stone ground organic loaf. But always choose any bread that has as little 'added' as possible. Watch out for preservatives and additives in processed packaged bread.
- Vary bread styles and flavours. I am a huge fan of good sourdough, but also enjoy a light wholemeal, chewy rye and grainy bread with lots of seeds and grains. Good bread changes your recipes!
- Storage: bread stales so if not using within a day or two at the most—cover tightly in a sealed bag and freeze (I like to portion out in smaller amounts, easy for reuse and keeps it all fresh).
- Defrost on a clean chopping board—it only takes several minutes. The microwave isn't always ideal—but be sure to use the lowest setting as often you will dry out the bread while defrosting it.
- Stale bread (or at least day old) is best for French toast, puddings and also making into fresh breadcrumbs.
- Warming bread to a crisp finish is a nice touch: simply pop it onto an oven tray. Give it a splash with water and bake 5 minutes in a 170°C (340°F) oven.

Eggs

Boiled Eggs

Serves 2

EQUIPMENT
heavy-based BIG saucepan, slotted spoon, and kitchen timer

INGREDIENTS
4 large free-range eggs, at room temperature
sea salt and freshly ground black pepper
toast, to serve (if desired —I like soldiers!)

METHOD
Have all the ingredients and equipment out before you begin.

Make sure your eggs are at room temperature by popping them into a large bowl and cover with some hot tap water for a few minutes before you begin cooking.

Choose a nice BIG saucepan even for two eggs!

Only cook eggs in a single layer. So if you are doing loads of eggs, you need a huge saucepan.

Bring the water to a gentle boil with even amounts of bubbles rising to the surface.

Put each egg on the spoon and lower them gently into the water one at a time. If you want the yolks centred, spin each egg as it's added to the pan.

Gently boil for 4 minutes for soft boiled (also known as coddled), 5 minutes for medium soft boiled (firm whites and runny yolk), 8 minutes for hard boiled and 9 minutes for very hard boiled.

Remove eggs with a slotted spoon and place into egg cups. Trim off the top, season with a touch of salt and pepper and serve with hot buttered toast (soldiers are my favourite).

Tip: For hard-boiled, pop them straight into some iced water or under a cold running tap for a few minutes when you take them out of the pan.

What went wrong

- Start with good-quality eggs, the best you can afford (cheapies don't have the taste, colour or important flavour you want).
- Cooking eggs straight from the fridge—eek. They are too cold and crack easily when popped into the water (little bits of the egg white will float through the water).
- Boiling too vigorously? The eggs knock into each other and crack and the high heat only encourages the white to be rubbery.
- Dark rings around your hard-boiled yolk? Remember to cool quickly under cold water or place into iced water immediately.
- Eggs that won't peel? They are not bad or off, just annoying. It usually means that your eggs are too fresh. Use them for perfect poached eggs instead and save your older eggs for hard boiling.

Fried Eggs

Serves 2

EQUIPMENT
small ramekin or jug, heavy-based non-stick frying pan with a lid, egg slide

INGREDIENTS
4 fresh free-range eggs
30g (1oz) butter and ½ teaspoon vegetable oil
sea salt

METHOD
Heat the frying pan over a medium heat for about a minute.

Add a little butter and oil to the pan and swirl to coat when butter is melted.

Crack one egg at a time into a small ramekin or jug.

Slide the egg gently into the pan, then repeat with the remaining eggs

Make sure there is room between each egg in the pan to prevent them sticking together.

As the edges begin to bubble and start to go golden, place the lid on the pan and cook until the eggs are done the way you like them. Remember not to overcook! The eggs will keep cooking a bit even once you take them out of the pan.

For flipped eggs (or over easy), run the egg slide around and under one egg and gently and confidently flip over, cooking lightly on the other side then carefully remove.

The perfect crisp or soft-bottomed friend to some crispy bacon, sautéed mushrooms or roasted tomatoes.

What went wrong

- Hard and rubbery whites? This is caused by overcooking or cooking in a pan that is much too hot or is too thin on the base.
- Broken yolk? Take care when cracking your eggs. If it's easier, crack them into a little dish or ramekin first and then slide them into the pan.
- Greasy and soggy eggs? They have been cooked in too much oil.

Omelette

Serves 2

EQUIPMENT

mixing bowl and balloon whisk or standmixer with whisk attachment, metric spoon measures, silicon spatula, heavy-based, good-quality, non-stick frying pan or purpose-made omelette or crepe pan

· ·

INGREDIENTS

2–4 fresh free-range eggs
2 tablespoons water (optional, some prefer omelettes made without)
sea salt flakes and freshly ground black pepper
knob (about 30g/1oz) butter
1 teaspoon olive or vegetable oil
optional extras: chopped ham, shredded cooked chicken, grated cheddar cheese, cooked sliced button mushrooms, fresh chopped herbs, diced tomato etc
toast or salad to serve

When you can 'whip up an omelette' you have mastered one of the classics! But it is not only about practice with this one it's very much about the frying pan.

METHOD

Have all the equipment out and ingredients weighed and measured.

Add the eggs and water (if using) to the mixing bowl. Whisk vigorously until well combined and bubbly.

Meanwhile heat a heavy-based non-stick pan over a medium high heat, adding the butter and oil. Heat until butter is foamy, swirling the pan to coat it with the mixture. Even when using a non-stick pan add the butter and oil for flavour and a golden colour.

Pour in the omelette mixture in one go.

Quickly, as soon as the omelette starts to set on the bottom (around 10 seconds), use a spatula to gently lift the outer edges of the omelette moving it to the inside of the pan. Continue to do this as it starts to cook through, allowing the egg mixture to fill in empty or thinly covered parts of the pan.

When the omelette is nearly set, scatter in the extras if using. Gently fold one side of the omelette over the other and slide the omelette out of the pan. Serve immediately.

Tip: The omelette will keep cooking so a little under is always better than a little over.

What went wrong

- Dry, overcooked, rubbery and tough? This is usually caused by cooking on too high heat for too long. And yes you can blame your tools—it's often partially caused by a bad pan. You need a heavy-based goodie here.
- Only add a little water to a basic omelette (no milk or cream). The water will evaporate to make the omelette soft and fluffy.
- Too much mixture? Work with a small amount of mixture, sticking to no more than 4 eggs. Omelettes are always best made small. You are usually better to make more than one using two pans if feeding the masses!
- Adding the mixture before the butter is 'foamy' tends to make it soggy and limp. Wait and be patient!
- Waiting too long to move the mixture in the pan. It's all very quick ... only about 10 seconds before the base starts to set.
- Moving the uncooked outside into the middle helps it cook evenly and stay fluffy and light.

Poached Eggs

Serves 2

EQUIPMENT

deep-frying pan (at least 5cm/2in) with a solid base but not too heavy, ramekin or small cup, slotted spoon

INGREDIENTS

4 of the freshest free-range eggs you can find (the best you can afford please!)
100ml (3½fl oz) white vinegar
sea salt flakes, freshly ground black pepper and gorgeous golden toast to serve

METHOD

Have all equipment out and ingredients ready. I also suggest the table is set or the plates are ready and waiting. If this is your first try, have someone else on toasting duties too!

Fill your pan about ¾ full with water. Add the vinegar.

Have a large deep bowl of warm water ready to pop the cooked poached eggs into. This is optional but I find this works well for me.

Heat the water over a medium heat. It's ready when there is a little steam and several bubbles appearing, but not boiling.

Crack an egg into the ramekin or cup. Stir the water to get a good whirlpool going and pop in the egg by bringing the ramekin down really close to the steaming water and sliding the egg in—be brave. The egg will turn and seal in a little neat package. Repeat with another egg, gently stirring the water in a small section of the pan and sliding the egg from the ramekin into the whirlpool.

Once white is set (about 3 minutes), remove the egg carefully with a slotted spoon and place into the bowl of water or lightly drain on the spoon and carefully place straight onto the hot, buttered toast.

For restaurant quality use a pair of kitchen scissors to trim away any egg strands to make a perfect round egg.

What went wrong

- Using old, stale eggs. Super fresh is the key! It will also help so much to have good quality eggs—the best you can afford.
- Not enough water or too many bubbles in the pan! If the water doesn't cover the egg it won't cook evenly. And too many bubbles will move the egg around breaking it up and losing the lovely little parcel shape.
- The wrong pan? If it's too shallow, there won't be enough water for your eggs to float. A pan that's too deep will make it hard to get your eggs in and out.
- Not stirring the water. Creating the "whirlpool" effect helps to give you a neat little parcel of egg. Just dropping it in can mean it will spread.
- Overcrowding the pan—four eggs at a time is really the absolute maximum. When starting out try one at a time.

Scrambled Eggs

Serves 2 to 3

EQUIPMENT

large mixing bowl, whisk (or standmixer with whisk attachment), metric measuring spoons, heavy-based, good quality, non-stick frying pan, silicon spatula or wooden spoon

INGREDIENTS

5 large free-range eggs

4–5 tablespoons cream or milk or water (water steams the eggs but the result is not as rich and creamy)

sea salt flakes, freshly ground black pepper

knob (about 30g/1oz) butter (if using a non-stick pan you can eliminate these, but I still use as it adds heaps of flavour)

optional extras: freshly chopped herbs (parsley, chives, basil, oregano etc), cheese (grated cheddar, crumbled feta or goat's cheese), semi-sundried tomatoes, smoked salmon, etc

METHOD

Add the eggs, cream (milk or water), and salt and pepper to the mixing bowl. Whisk vigorously until well combined and bubbly.

Meanwhile, heat the frying pan over a medium heat with the butter or oil. When butter is foamy add the egg mixture in one go to the pan. If adding any extras, like herbs, scatter these into the pan now.

Gently stir and lightly fold the mixture from the outside inwards, without over mixing. I like my eggs in large, just firm curds.

Serve immediately with your favourite buttered toast.

Tip: The eggs will continue cooking a little once out of the pan.

A standby meal that's so perfect just about anytime... breakfast, brunch, lunch or supper

What went wrong

- Adding too much liquid to the eggs: maximum of 1 tablespoon of milk, cream or water for each whole large egg.

- Too much mixture in the pan! This causes overcooking. Keep it to 4 serves, which is around 8 eggs. If you have more to feed, use two pans and do separate batches.

- A lightweight pan: eggs will easily scorch and burn.

- Overstirring! This causes the curds to shrink and become hard and rubbery.

- OVERCOOKING! This causes curds to push out liquid. Eeek! Watery scrambled eggs!

Whipping

EQUIPMENT

flat-bladed knife or palette knife, selection of bowls (two for separating eggs and a large mixing bowl for the whipping), standmixer with whisk or electric hand beaters

Tip: To whip by hand you will need the equipment above and a metal balloon whisk. Placing a dry cloth under your bowl will help keep it stable.

. . . .

INGREDIENTS

large free-range eggs at room temperature (not too fresh!)

METHOD

Allow eggs to come to room temperature, about 30 minutes out of the fridge OR place eggs into a bowl of warm water for 10 minutes, drain and gently dry with a soft cloth.

Make sure the mixing bowls and whisks are sparkling clean and completely dry. A little lemon juice or vinegar dabbed onto a soft dry cloth and wiped around the bowls makes sure they are oil-free.

Extra bowls. I suggest three. I think it always pays to separate the egg into two smaller bowls (one for the white and one for the yolk), before you transfer the whites into your whipping bowl. This will ensure you can inspect for any cheeky bits of yolk before adding. Remember NO yolk in the white AT ALL! However, it doesn't matter if there is a little white in the yolk. Often when you rush and do not bother with the extra bowl method you will break a yolk and three or four egg whites end up with yolk in them. Take your time and do it carefully to ensure success!

Separate eggs (see next point) slowly and patiently.

To separate, tap the egg on its side with a flat-bladed knife. Cracking the egg on the side of a bowl often is uneven and helps the egg yolk break straight away. Open the egg into two halves and slowly tip the yolk from one half of the shell into the other, back and forth. Have a bowl underneath to collect the egg white and a separate bowl for the egg yolks.

Restaurant method: for those who don't mind a little food on their hands. Gently crack the egg on its side with a flat-bladed knife. Prise open shell and tip egg into your cupped, CLEAN and dry hand, allowing the white to run through your fingers into the collection bowl. Slide the yolk into its own bowl.

Removing a little shell from the whites: the best method is to use the edge of the egg shell.

Add a pinch of salt (or for a sweeter meringue a pinch of cream of tartar) to the whites just before whipping. This will help to keep the egg white firm and improve the volume.

SOFT PEAKS

Add the whisk to the whites and beat on high speed. The eggs will initially look foamy and translucent. Quickly they become white and will form a SOFT peak that falls back on itself when the whisk is lifted. Soft peaks are the best stage to use when folding into other mixtures, such as cakes and mousses.

FIRM PEAKS

Continue beating and whisking past the soft peak stage, lifting the whisk often to check the strength of the peak formed. Firm peaks are quite stiff, very white and will hold their shape when lifted with the whisk. Firm peaks are often the stage required before sugar is added in many meringue recipes.

OVER-BEATEN WHITES

The egg white peaks and then quickly becomes granular and separates, releasing a liquid that sits on top. Throw away and start again!

What went wrong

- Eggs straight from the fridge will be too cold and will not aerate properly when you are whipping the egg whites.
- Egg yolk intruder! When separating your whites from your yolks, allowing even the tiniest bit of yolk into the white will ruin your whipping.
- Wet or oily bowls or beater! Your bowls and equipment must be clean, clean, clean and dry, dry, dry!
- Under or overbeating. Watch and take note! Overbeating will cause it to separate and become grainy as well as removing all the air from the beginning of the beating. Underbeating will not add enough air and leave your end result much flatter than you would hope for!
- Not using immediately! Leaving your whipped whites unattended for a time will see them flop every time!

Bread

Bread & Butter Pudding

Serves 4

EQUIPMENT

scales and/or metric measuring cups, measuring spoons, measuring jug, butter knife, 1.5 litre (3 pint) ovenproof dish, medium saucepan, standmixer or beaters

· ·

INGREDIENTS

60g (2oz) butter, softened to room temperature

8 thick slices day-old bread (at least 1cm/¹/₃in thick and preferably hand cut)

350ml (12fl oz) full-cream milk

250ml (9fl oz) cream

4 eggs (at room temperature)

3 tablespoons caster (superfine) sugar

1 teaspoon vanilla extract

1 teaspoon finely grated orange rind (optional)

1 teaspoon ground cinnamon

When done well it's gorgeous, gooey and oh so comforting—not to mention a great use for leftover bread.

METHOD

Preheat the oven to 180°C (350°F). Grease your oven dish well with butter.

Butter the bread (going right to the very edges) with a butter knife, taking care not to tear the bread. Cut the bread in half diagonally.

Arrange the bread slices over the bottom of the dish, overlapping.

Place the milk, cream, sugar, vanilla and orange rind If using) into a medium-sized saucepan and heat over a low heat until just warmed. Pour into the mixing bowl on your mixer or into a large mixing bowl with the eggs. Use the whisk attachment of your electric beaters and beat on medium for about 1 minute or until the mixture is very bubbly and foamy.

Drizzle the still warm custard all over the bread. Sprinkle with cinnamon and stand for 5 minutes so the bread soaks up a little of the custard.

Bake on the centre shelf for 30–35 minutes or until the bread is golden brown and lightly crisp, and the custard is firm. Be careful not to overbake.

Tip: Warming the mixture allows the bread to soak it up, This produces a soft inside to the bread yet delicious crisp golden top.

What went wrong

- Incorrect measuring. Too much milk will bring you undone every time. Follow the recipe for success!
- Not enough custard! Your bread will be dry and have none of that lovely, oozy, gooey texture!
- Incorrect oven temperature! Too high and the bread surface will burn or overcook, producing weepy liquid. Too low and you'll be there forever!
- The wrong bread! Too thin and the bread just falls apart in the custard and the pudding is soggy. It must be just right!
- Fresh bread. It will fall apart instantly. For beautiful results always use, at least, day-old bread.

Croutons

2 cups croutons

EQUIPMENT

chopping board, serrated knife, large heavy-based frying pan, tongs, paper towel

INGREDIENTS

½ loaf day-old bread, crusts removed, cut into dice approx 1.5 x 1.5cm (¾ x ¾in)
125ml (4fl oz) pure olive oil
sea salt flakes

METHOD

Use day-old bread.

Cut into even-sized cubes or slices for a baguette.

Heat the oil over a medium heat to just hot. Add one small cube and check the bread sizzles before adding the rest.

Cook in one layer only, gently occasionally tossing with tongs and or shaking the pan.

Drain on paper towel and toss with salt flakes. Repeat with remaining bread cubes.

The essential finishing ingredient to add a little more love and crunch to your soups or salads.

What went wrong

- Greasy croutons? You've used too much oil. amd the croutons have soaked it up.
- Adding bread when oil is not hot enough.
- Overcrowding the pan.
- Burning oil and bread.
- Not draining on paper towel can make the croutons go soggy.

French Toast

Serves 2–4

EQUIPMENT
serrated/bread knife, chopping board, standmixer with whisk attachment, shallow sided dish (large enough to fit bread slice in), heavy-based frying pan, egg slide, large plate

INGREDIENTS
½ unsliced loaf good quality white crusty bread
1/3 cup (75g/2½oz) caster (superfine) sugar
3 large free range eggs, at room temperature
50ml (1¾fl oz) milk
50g (1¾oz) butter
3 tablespoons caster (superfine) sugar and ½ teaspoon ground cinnamon, mixed together on a plate
maple syrup and/or berries, to serve (optional)

METHOD
Slice the bread with a serrated knife into 2 cm thick slices (don't be tempted to use thin slices) or buy good quality thick sliced bread.

Place the sugar, eggs and milk into the bowl of your standmixer with the whisk attachment. Whisk on medium low (speed 4) for 20 seconds until bubbly and aerated. Pour the mixture into the shallow sided dish.

Add the slices of bread. Let soak for 1 minute then carefully turn over and soak the other side for 30 seconds.

Meanwhile, heat the frying pan over a medium heat until hot then add the butter. Lift the bread slices from the mixture (carefully with a egg lifter) and add to the hot foamy butter.

Turn the heat down to low (don't let the bread burn) and cook for 2 minutes or until golden brown. Turn over (carefully, with the egg lifter) and cook until golden. Repeat with remaining bread.

Coat with the extra cinnamon sugar and serve with maple syrup and berries.

SAVOURY VERSION
Add ½ teaspoon ground cumin and or curry powder to the egg mix and omit all the sugar. Serve sprinkled with sea salt and freshly ground black pepper and tomato sauce or a relish..

What went wrong

- Bread that's too thin and too fresh! Your toast won't absorb the egg and will not be soft and fluffy in the middle.
- Too little or too much soaking of bread in egg mixture. It will either be dry and flavourless or soggy!
- Frying pan incorrect temperature ... too hot and the bread will burn and inside will be cold and not be cooked through; too cold and it will be soggy and runny.
- Too much turning and poking! This will make your French toast flatter and could cause it to break. Be gentle and ideally just turn once or twice.
- Too much butter makes greasy and oily French toast.

Garlic Bread

Serves 4

EQUIPMENT

Chopping board, serrated knife, food processor with small bowl (or mixing bowl and wooden spoon), measuring spoons, scales, flat-bladed knife or small spatula for spreading, foil, baking tray

INGREDIENTS

175g (6oz) unsalted or reduced salt butter, softened to room temperature (using regular butter often makes garlic bread too salty)

1½ tablespoons extra virgin olive oil (this adds a richness and spreadable consistency to the butter)

pinch sea salt (if using unsalted butter)

3–4 cloves garlic (preferably locally grown)

½ cup chopped herbs such as parsley or chives or combination

2 good-quality, medium-sized baguettes (such as sourdough or a good crispy French style)

METHOD

Choose good, crusty, dense bread.

Cut with a serrated knife nearly all the way through leaving just the bottom together.

Cut slices 2–2.5cm (¾–1in) thick.

Use a food processor to combine the garlic, herbs, butter and oil to a creamy smooth butter.

Spread the garlic butter on both sides of the bread and a little all over the top of the loaf. Do not drown the bread in garlic butter.

Wrap in foil, securing well and place on a baking tray. Bake in a moderate oven, about 180°C (350°F) for about 15 minutes. Open foil and bake uncovered for 7 minutes or until lightly golden and crisp. The bread can also be cooked on the barbecue plate. Cook covered, turning often, for about 12–15 minutes.

Why do we all love garlic bread? Serve anytime as a starter or with a main meal. For a gluten-free option use a gluten-free baguette.

What went wrong

- The wrong type of bread, not too light and fluffy, or it soaks up the butter and becomes oily. Or it can become dry if the buttering is insufficient.
- Dried or bottled chopped garlic—this can taste too strong and causes garlic breath. Choose fresh and preferably locally grown, organic.
- Garlic that is chopped too chunky. Make sure it is very finely chopped so that the garlic cooks.
- Too little or too much garlic butter, making the bread dry or soggy.
- Oven too hot and not wrapping bread stick in foil. This can burn the bread.

Simple White Loaf

Makes 1 (800g/28oz cooked) loaf (recipe can be doubled if desired to make two loaves)

EQUIPMENT

scales and or measuring cups, liquid cup measure, measuring spoons, standmixer with beater and dough hook, clean tea towel, baking tray, cooks knife, cooling rack

. . . .

INGREDIENTS

550g (19oz) strong bread flour
7g (2½ teaspoons) dried yeast
2 teaspoons sugar
1 teaspoon salt flakes
300ml (10½fl oz) warm water
1 tablespoon olive oil
extra oil and a little flour

Homemade bread is a joy to make, smell and eat ... you could be surprised at how simple it is.

METHOD

Place the flour, yeast, sugar, salt (all the dried ingredients) into the mixing bowl of your standmixer with the beater attachment, turn to low speed (1) and mix 10 seconds or until combined.

Add the water and oil, while the mixer is turning. Mix for a further 15 seconds or until a dough begins to just form. Change to the hook/kneading attachment.

Knead on low speed (1) for 5 minutes or until the dough is smooth and soft (it will also 'spring back' when pressed with your fingertip).

Lightly oil a large bowl (you can use the bowl from the standmixer—just give it a good wipe). Place the dough into the bowl and cover with a clean tea towel. Place in a warm (but not hot), draft-free place. Allow to stand at least 1–1½ hours or until the dough doubles in size.

Return the dough to the standmixer, with the kneading/dough hook attachment and mix 10 seconds (this can also be called 'punching down').

Sprinkle some flour onto a baking tray. Form the dough into a round 'cob' shaped loaf and place on the floured tray. Set aside in the same warm place, covered with a clean tea towel, for around 30 minutes to prove again.

Preheat the oven to 220°C (420°F).

Scatter the top of the loaf with a little extra flour and quickly slash the top a couple of times. Bake the bread for 10 minutes, then reduce the temperature to 200°C (400°F) and bake a further 20 minutes or until golden and the bread sounds hollow when tapped on the base.

What went wrong

- Not weighing ingredients properly. The ratio of dry ingredients, water and oil is very important.
- Not using high-protein/strong flour—you need the additional protein/gluten for structure and lift.
- Stale or not enough yeast. I recommend freeze-dried yeast as it is very easy to use and has a long shelf life.
- Too much sugar or salt—this will kill and inactivate the yeast.
- Water that's too hot—the water must be tepid, which is just warm or the heat will kill the yeast.
- Standing the dough in a cold or drafty spot. Find a warm place out of a draft. I usually pop mine by the kitchen window, or close to the oven on a cold day—the sun or warmth helps the dough to rise.
- Not enough kneading—allow the standmixer to knead the dough slowly. The dough must be smooth and springy. The slow speed is needed to produce gluten, which will give the bread lightness and a good texture.

Homemade Pizza Base

Makes 1 medium to large base

EQUIPMENT
scales and/or measuring cups, measuring spoons, liquid measuring jug, standmixer with beater and dough hook, clean tea towel, rolling pin, pizza tray or baking sheet

. . . .

INGREDIENTS
250g (9oz) strong high protein flour (I really like Italian '00' flour for pizza)
2 teaspoons dried yeast
1½ teaspoons sugar
1 teaspoon salt
40ml (1½fl oz) olive oil
100–125ml (3½–4fl oz) warm water (not too cold and definitely NOT hot—technically around 41°C/106°F)
a little extra flour for rolling and dusting the bench

Recipe can be doubled.

Once you master this, storebought pizza just won't seem as good ever again.

METHOD

Weigh the ingredients correctly.

Place the flour, yeast, sugar and salt into the mixing bowl of your standmixer. Using the beater attachment mix on slow (speed 1) for 10 seconds or until combined. Add the oil and nearly all of the water (hold back on the last tablespoon as you may not need it). Mix for 15 seconds on slow (speed 1) until the mixture comes together to a rough dough. If the mixture looks dry, add the remaining water.

Change to the dough hook and knead on slow (speed 1) for 5 minutes or until the dough is silky smooth and soft.

Form into a ball. Place into a clean bowl and lightly oil it (you can use the mixing bowl to the standmixer—just give it a wipe out with a clean dry cloth first). Cover lightly with a clean tea towel and place in a warm draft free place for 1 hour or until dough doubles in size.

Preheat the oven to 220°C (420°F). Lightly oil your pizza tray or baking sheet.

Lightly dust the bench with a little flour and knead the dough once or twice until smooth. Roll out with the rolling pin to the size of your pizza tray.

Top with your favourite tomato paste or passata* and your choice of cheese and toppings. Bake 20–30 minutes or until crisp and golden.

Tip: The pizza base can be precooked for 5 minutes then cooled, covered well with plastic film and frozen for up to three months or refrigerated for up to five days.

*Passata is pureed tomatoes that is sold in a large jar at supermarkets and delis.

What went wrong

- Over-proving (the dough will be spongy and too thick).
- Not weighing ingredients properly. The ratio of dry ingredients, water and oil is very important.
- Not using high protein/strong flour (you need the additional protein/gluten for structure and lift).
- Stale or not enough yeast. I recommend freeze-dried yeast as it is very easy to use and has a long shelf life.
- Too much sugar or salt—this will kill and inactivate the yeast.
- The water is too hot—the water must be tepid, which is just warm or the heat will kill the yeast.
- Standing the dough is a cold or drafty spot—find a warm place out of a draft. I usually pop mine by the kitchen window, or close to the oven on a cold day—the sun or warmth helps the dough to rise..
- Not enough kneading. Allow the standmixer to knead the dough slowly. The dough must be smooth and springy. The slow speed is needed to produce gluten, which will give the pizza base lightness and a good texture.

Toad in the Hole

Serves 2-4

EQUIPMENT
toaster or oven grill, chopping board, glass or cutter about 6cm (2¹/₃in) size, large heavy-based frying pan, egg slide

INGREDIENTS
4 slices your favourite bread
4 large free-range eggs
50g (1¾oz) butter
sea salt flakes and freshly ground black pepper
tomato sauce (optional)

METHOD
Toast the bread lightly first.

Leave on the crusts (they give extra support and prevent the egg yolk from breaking).

Cut a medium-sized hole out directly in the centre of the bread.

Melt the butter in the pan over a medium heat and lightly fry the bread, gently turning it over once.

Crack the egg open down close to the hole and gently place the egg in.

Cook gently, covering partially with a lid if desired until the egg is cooked to your liking.

Repeat with remaining toast and eggs, don't overcrowd the frying pan. Or use two frying pans!

The dish my husband always made for the children when they were little and they loved it! Called frog in the hole by some.

What went wrong

- Cracking the egg from up too high so it breaks or misses the hole and spills out!
- Undercooking the egg so you get oozy white bits.
- Turning or flipping, which will cause running and the egg to overcook and become rubbery and yuk!
- Using untoasted bread.
- Adding the egg to the bread before it's in the pan—oops!
- Pan too hot? You could burn the eggs or the bread.
- Too much butter or oil? The toad in the hole will be greasy and oily.
- Overcrowding the pan will take the heat from the pan so your bread won't crisp and brown and it makes it too hard to flip the toast.

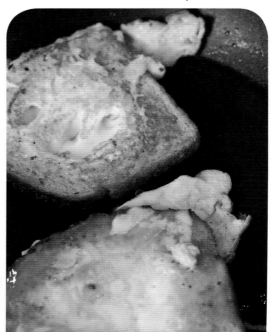

Toasted Sandwiches

Serves 2-4

EQUIPMENT

chopping board, bread knife, butter knife, serrated knife, cheese grater, heavy-based, non-stick frying pan, egg slide

INGREDIENTS

loaf of good quality sliced bread (white, sourdough or whole grain—fresh or day old)
softened butter for spreading
knob butter (30g/1oz) for the pan
2 teaspoons olive oil
4 slices of your favourite ham
4 evenly cut slices of your favourite melting cheese (like cheddar or Swiss)

METHOD

Butter two slices of bread lightly on both sides of the bread (or if preferred only on the 'outside' of the slices where it is going to touch the pan).

Lay the ham and cheese on the inside of one piece of bread and top with the other slice. Remember the outsides must be buttered!

Heat the pan over a medium low heat adding the butter and a little oil. The oil will help stop the butter burning. When the butter is just melted and starting to foam a little, carefully add the sandwich with the egg slide.

Allow to cook gently until golden underneath. Carefully and slowly turn over with the egg slide and cook the other side until golden. Cooking gently ensures the bread browns and the filling warms. If the cheese is not melted, turn down the heat and keep turning over regularly to allow it to keep cooking through without burning the outside.

Serve immediately. Repeat the process if making more than one sandwich keeping the others warm on a plate and covered loosely with foil or get a couple of pans on the go!

Before sandwich makers, this was the preferred method—golden fried, lightly crisp with a soft oozy centre. It's the perfect snack.

What went wrong

- The wrong bread. Thin and flavourless! No white fluff here please!
- Too much or too little cheese and filling. The ratio of bread to filling has to be just right!
- Over-turning and squashing.
- Pan too hot! This will give you an outside that is hard and sometimes burnt with a cold inside.
- Adding the sandwich to the pan too soon. If the pan is too cold your sandwich will soak up the butter and become soggy and oily!

Potatoes

Chips

Serves 4

EQUIPMENT

scales, potato peeler, cook's knife, paper towel or clean tea towel, large saucepan, wok or deep fryer, slotted spoon or frying spatula, oven rack and oven tray

INGREDIENTS

1.5 kg (3lb 5oz) potatoes (best results with King Edward, Binge or Russel Burbank; otherwise try Desiree or Sebago)
2 litres (4.2 pints) vegetable oil
sea salt
white vinegar or tomato sauce to serve (if desired)

METHOD

Buy the correct potato for chips and frying.

Peel the potatoes and cut into uniform lengths and sizes.

Dry potatoes with paper towel or a clean tea towel and cover lightly.

Fill a deep saucepan to no more than half full (maximum) with clean vegetable oil.

Preheat the oven to 200°C (400°F). Place the rack over the baking tray and set aside until needed.

Heat the oil over a medium heat until 190°C (375°F). Test with a thermometer or add a little cube of bread to the oil and if it sizzles the oil is ready. Remove and discard bread.

Divide the chips into three batches. Cook the first batch for about 5–7 minutes or until the chips just start to colour. Remove with the slotted spoon and lightly drain on paper towel then place on the rack over the tray. Place the tray into the oven.

Repeat with the second and third batches of chips as above.

Cook in the oven until golden and brown. Serve with sea salt, vinegar and or tomato sauce.

Tip: The chips can be cooked for 5 minutes only then set aside. When ready to serve reheat oil and fry until golden brown, but remember not to overfill the pan.

What went wrong

- The incorrect potato for frying (best to use an all purpose or waxy variety).
- Overcrowding the pan—this reduces the temperature of the oil and will mean the chips soak up the oil and become soggy.
- Oil not hot enough, so chips go soggy.
- Oil too hot? Chips will be burnt on the outside but raw in the middle.
- Dirty oil—this leaves specks all over the chip.

Roasted Potatoes

Serves 4

EQUIPMENT

scales, chopping board, cook's knife, potato peeler, saucepan with lid, fork, roasting pan, tongs

INGREDIENTS

1.5kg (3lb 5oz) King Edward, Russel Burbank, Kipfler or Sebago potatoes
50ml (1¾ oz) olive oil or vegetable oil
sea salt

METHOD

Choose the right potato. Have all the ingredients ready.

Preheat the oven to 200°C (400°F). Line a roasting pan with a big sheet of baking paper (this prevents sticking and burning).

Peel the potato and cut in half if large.

Place the potatoes into a saucepan and cover with water. Bring to the boil and cook for 8 minutes or until about half cooked. Drain well. Return potatoes to the saucepan and cook, shaking the pan over a dry heat to dry out all moisture. The shaking around in the pan will also rough up the edges.

Take a fork and scrape the edges to 'rough' them up a little more (this makes them super crispy when roasting).

Add the oil to the saucepan and toss the potatoes to coat them lightly.

Transfer the potatoes to the roasting pan and place into the oven.

Roast for 50 minutes, turning during the cooking until the potatoes are crispy on the outside and soft and fluffy on the inside. Sprinkle with salt flakes to serve.

The essential ingredient for making the perfect roast dinner.

What went wrong

- Choosing the incorrect potato—not too floury, but not too waxy (I like to use good old Sebago, Desiree, or specialty potatoes like Russel Burbank or Kipfler).
- Roasting in too-low heat (this just causes the potatoes to soak up the oil and fall apart).
- Cooking in too much oil (really this is frying the potatoes, you only want to toss them in oil).

Hash Browns

Serves 4

EQUIPMENT

food processor or large hand grater, scales, vegetable peeler (optional), large fine sieve, clean tea towels, 2 mixing bowls, large non-stick frying pan, egg slide, paper towel

INGREDIENTS

600g (21oz) Sebago potatoes (or an all-purpose potato), washed and dried (you do not have to peel them—that's too much effort!)
60ml (2fl oz) vegetable oil
sea salt

METHOD

Coarsely grate the potatoes in a food processor or by hand.

Line a large fine sieve or colander with a clean tea towel and add the grated potato. Pull up the sides and firmly squeeze as much liquid from the potatoes as possible. Open and season with plenty of salt and pepper. Cover again until ready to cook. Keep covered (the potato will quickly discolour).

Heat the oil in a large non-stick pan, add about ¼ cup amounts of the potato mixture, pressing gently with an egg slide. Cook over a medium heat for about 8 minutes or until golden brown and crisp underneath. Do not flip too early as the potatoes will stick.

Flip over carefully and cook the other side until golden brown and crispy.

Tip: Don't overcrowd the pan. Use two pans at once for a larger quantity.

My son Harry's very favourite snack! Thanks Katie for this family favourite.

What went wrong

- Choosing the incorrect potato. Not too waxy please)
- Not squeezing out enough liquid from the potatoes (they will be wet and fall apart).
- Overcrowding the pan.
- Oil too hot (hash browns will burn and be raw inside).
- Oil too cold (they will soak it up and become soggy and greasy).

Mashed Potatoes

Serves 4

EQUIPMENT

*scales, potato peeler, cook's knife, chopping board, medium-sized
saucepan, lid (optional), colander, potato masher, liquid measuring cup,
small saucepan or microwave safe bowl*

INGREDIENTS

*1.5kg (3lb 5oz) floury potatoes (such as Sebago, Dutch Creams, King
Edwards, Spunta or Desiree)*
60g (2oz) butter
125ml (4fl oz) milk or cream

METHOD

Choose a floury potato.

Peel and cut into large even-sized pieces.

Place into salted water—only just cover with water by about 2cm (¾in),
do not drown the potatoes!

Partially cover the pot with a lid, if desired, and bring to the boil.
Reduce the heat and simmer for about 15 minutes or until potatoes are
tender when tested with a knife.

For really creamy mash: Place the milk, butter and or cream in a small
saucepan and heat until just steaming. Do not boil!

Tip the potatoes into a colander and drain before returning to the
saucepan. Mash with a masher, then beat in the hot milk mixture. Season
with salt and pepper to taste.

*Tip: You can also place hot potatoes with the milk mixture into
your standmixer and beat for around 1 minute. Be careful not to
overbeat. Do not use a food processor.*

What went wrong

- Processing in a food processor. This results in
a gluey stringy mash.
- Choosing the incorrect potato for mashing.
Floury potatoes are best, anything too waxy
will not mash to a fluffy soft creamy result.
- Cutting the potatoes into irregular shapes.
They just won't cook evenly—some will be
undercooked, causing lumps, and some will
be overcooked and waterlogged.
- Too much water can drown the potatoes
(just cover and simmer).
- Overcooking! The potatoes fall apart in the
water.
- Mashing with too much butter or milk.
(ruins the texture).

Perfect Boiled Potatoes

Serves 4-6

EQUIPMENT

scales, medium sized saucepan with tight-fitting lid, colander, tongs, chopping board, cook's knife

INGREDIENTS

1.5kg (3lb 5oz) chat potatoes (small Coliban variety potatoes)
50g (1¾oz) butter
sea salt and fresh ground black pepper
½ cup freshly chopped parsley and chives

METHOD

Place the whole potatoes into the saucepan and just cover with water. Add a good pinch of salt.

Bring to the boil. Cover with the lid and turn off the heat. Allow to stand for 20 minutes (see Tip).

Test the potatoes are tender with the tip of a knife. If too firm return to the boil and simmer very gently until tender.

Drain potatoes carefully into a colander. Cut or slice if desired.

Return gently to the saucepan and toss carefully with butter and herbs and season to taste with salt and pepper.

Serve immediately.

Tip: Standing the potatoes in the hot water produces a tender soft result without any waterlogging or skin falling off.

The simplicity and flavour of a perfectly boiled whole potato, tossed in a little butter with fresh chopped herbs is delicious.

What went wrong

- The wrong choice of potato for boiling. Don't choose floury varieties as they will fall apart and become waterlogged.
- Incorrectly sized saucepan and too much water.
- Potatoes cut into irregular sizes—they will never cook at the same time! Of course this doesn't apply if you are using whole baby chat potatoes!
- Boiling too vigorously—be kind to your taties!
- Waterlogged and falling apart? This is from cooking the potatoes in too much water and using a floury potato variety.

Scalloped Potatoes

Serves 4-6

EQUIPMENT
Scales and/or measuring cups, liquid cup measure, vegetable peeler, 2-litre oven-proof baking dish, food processor with slicing and grating discs (or a sharp knife, hand grater, mixing jug and whisk)

INGREDIENTS
1.5kg (3lb 5oz) old potatoes (such as Sebago or an all-purpose potato)
250ml (9fl oz) cream
200ml (7fl oz) milk
good pinch each of sea salt, cinnamon and nutmeg
150g (5oz) cheddar cheese
freshly ground black pepper

METHOD
Grease your oven dish well with butter. Preheat the oven to 200°C (400°F).

Peel the potatoes and slice in your food processor with the slicing disc or by hand with a sharp knife.

Layer in dish, overlapping slightly.

Pop the cream, milk and seasonings into the processor and pulse until combined or mix together in a large jug with a whisk. Pour this savoury custard over the potato slices. Rinse and dry the food processor bowl if using.

Use the grating disc in the food processor or your hand grater to coarsely grate the cheese. Set aside.

Bake uncovered for 1 hour on the middle shelf of the oven. Scatter over the grated cheese and bake for 30–40 minutes more or until potatoes are tender and cheese is bubbly and golden.

What went wrong

- Choosing the incorrect potato! Floury potatoes are best, or even an all-purpose potato, anything too waxy will not soften to a delicious soft bake.
- Unevenly sliced potato! This will result in pieces being undercooked or overcooked. We want them ALL just right!
- Too much milk! The potatoes won't absorb excess liquid especially if you use the wrong variety.
- Incorrect heat! Too low and the dish will not cook becoming soggy, or too high and the cream mixture will curdle and the potatoes on the surface will dry out.

Rice

Baked Rice Pudding

Serves 4

EQUIPMENT

baking tray, scales or measuring cups, liquid measuring jug, 1.5 litre (3 pint) ovenproof baking dish, large spoon or spatula

INGREDIENTS

50g (1¾oz) flaked almonds
400ml (14fl oz) full-cream milk
500ml (17½fl oz) cream
1 cup (approx. 225g/8oz) arborio or short/medium grain rice
⅓ cup ((75g/2½ oz) caster (superfine) sugar
2 teaspoons vanilla extract
ground cinnamon

Recipe can be halved or doubled if desired.

METHOD

Weigh and measure all the ingredients

   Preheat oven to 170°C (340°F) and grease a 1.5 litre (52fl oz) ovenproof dish.

   Grease a sheet of foil and set aside.

   Scatter the almonds on the baking dish and roast 7 minutes or until golden. Set aside.

   Put the milk, cream, rice, sugar and vanilla into the dish. Stir combining all the ingredients. Cover with foil, securing to the sides of the dish.

   Bake for 1 hour 15 minutes, covered. Remove the foil and bake uncovered for a further 15 minutes or until lightly browned. Stand 10 minutes before serving topped with almonds.

Tip: For extra naughtiness ... serve drizzled with cream. Yum!

What went wrong

- Using the incorrect rice (short or medium grain only).
- Too much sugar! Too sweet and will cause burning.
- Overcooking or not covering during the baking.
- Baking on a high temperature! Resulting in dried-out, over-cooked, horrible pud.

Fried Rice

Serves 2-4

EQUIPMENT

chopping board, cook's knife, vegetable peeler, bowls for separating the ingredients, large spatula or wok charn, wok or large, deep frying pan

. . . .

INGREDIENTS

2 cloves garlic

3cm (1¹/₃in) fresh ginger, peeled

6 spring onions (scallions), tops discarded

1 medium carrot, peeled

1 red capsicum (bell pepper), halved and seeds discarded

350g (12oz) Chinese roast pork or roast duck or chicken

3 cups cold long grain cooked rice (preferably refrigerated overnight)

2 large eggs

good pinch salt

4–5 tablespoons peanut or vegetable oil

½ cup frozen peas

SAUCE

2 tablespoons soy sauce, 1 tablespoon Chinese rice wine, 2 teaspoons caster (superfine) sugar, several drops sesame oil

Recipe can be halved or doubled if desired.

Begin with well-cooked Steamed Rice (see recipe) then grab a large wok or deep frying pan and you're off..

METHOD

Measure and weigh out all ingredients.

Finely chop the garlic, ginger and spring onions—place into one bowl. Dice the carrot and capsicum into tiny dice and pop into another bowl.

Chop the pork or shred the duck or chicken into bite-sized pieces and place into a separate bowl.

Break up the rice with your fingers, separating any lumps.

Whisk the eggs with the salt until foamy.

Heat a wok or deep frying pan over a high heat. Add about 1 tablespoon of the oil to the wok and swirl. When slightly smoking, pour in the eggs in one go and move around the wok to make a thin bubbly airy pancake. Flip over with the wok charn or spatula and cook the other side. Remove from the wok and shred into bite sized strips. Set aside.

Add 2 teaspoons of the oil to the pan; add the garlic, ginger and spring onions; lightly toss and stirfry for 30 seconds. Remove from the wok. Add 1 tablespoon oil to the wok and heat, add the carrot and capsicum and toss 1 minute; remove from wok add to the spring onions.

Add 2 teaspoons oil to the wok and reheat. Add the pork, toss 1 minute, remove from wok. Add the remaining oil and heat. Add the rice to the wok and cook, tossing for 2 minutes or until heated through. (Make sure the heat is still high when you add the rice so that you can always hear a big sizzling sound as it cooks!)

Return all the ingredients to the pan and toss well. Combine the sauce ingredients and toss through the rice. Serve immediately.

What went wrong

- Rice stuck together and stodgy? This is caused by using warm or freshly cooked rice.
- Cooking in the wrong pan—it's best to use a carbon steel wok otherwise the rice can stick, burn or go gluggy.
- Overloading the pan or wok will cause overcooking and stewing instead of frying—gluggy, gluggy!
- Overcooking the added-in vegetables makes them mushy and lose their colour and texture.
- Overseasoning—always taste to avoid making it too salty or acidic. Flavours should be balanced.

Simple Pilaf

Serves 4

EQUIPMENT

chopping board, cook's knife, liquid measuring jug, 2 large heavy-based saucepans (with well fitting lids), scales, fine grater, wooden spoon, fork

INGREDIENTS

700ml (24fl oz) good chicken or vegetable stock
40g (1½oz) butter
1 tablespoon olive oil
1 small onion, finely chopped
1 clove garlic, finely chopped
600g (21oz) basmati rice (1 cup = 235g)
125ml (4oz) dry white wine or vermouth
grated rind and juice 1 lemon
½ cup fresh chopped parsley
2 spring onions, finely chopped
1 cup baby spinach leaves
sea salt and freshly ground black pepper

METHOD

Bring the stock to the boil in one of the saucepans and partially cover with a lid, keeping the stock HOT.

Melt the butter and oil in a big, heavy-based saucepan until foamy. Add the onion and garlic, and cook over a medium heat until softened.

Add the rice and stir well to coat in the butter. Cook 1 minute or until glossy.

Stir in the wine and stir well until evaporated. Add the stock in one go and pop on a tight-fitting lid.

Reduce the heat to very, very low and cook for 10 minutes. Remove from the heat (do not take off the lid) and set aside for 10 minutes.

Remove the lid, pop over the heat for one quick burst. Add the spring onions, spinach and herbs, lemon zest and juice. Season with salt and pepper and fluff up with a fork.

What went wrong

- Using a medium short grain rice—long grain is best
- Using cold stock—it will not absorb quickly and pilaf will end up gluggy.
- Using a saucepan that is too thin—always use a heavy-based saucepan or it will stick and burn on the bottom before the rice cooks through.
- Cooking over a high heat—the bottom will burn before the rice is cooked.
- Taking the lid off too soon. Always allow the rice to stand before serving—no peeking please!

Pumpkin Risotto

Serves 4

EQUIPMENT

*chopping board, cook's knife, liquid measuring jug, 2 x
saucepans (one large, one medium), ladle, wooden spoon,
scales, fine grater*

. . . .

INGREDIENTS

*1.5 litres (6 cups/52fl oz) good vegetable or chicken stock (if
using packaged stock I prefer salt reduced, as many brands
are too salty)*
500ml (2 cups/17½fl oz) dry white wine
50g (1¾oz) butter
3 tablespoons olive oil
1 small onion, finely diced
1 stick celery, finely diced
300g (10½oz) pumpkin, peeled and cut into bite-sized pieces
600g (3 cups) arborio rice
100g (3½oz) parmesan, freshly grated
50g (1¾oz) butter, extra or ½ cup thickened cream
freshly chopped parsley and extra grated parmesan to serve

*Tips: Be ready to stand and stir in between each batch
of stock. Choose the best, heaviest-based saucepan
you have or the risotto will stick and burn. There are
methods where you don't have to stir constantly, but
work on the real method first.*

*If using chicken, use diced thigh meat. Add seafood
at the end of the cooking and simply stir through. The
heat within the risotto will cook it or, if preferred, the
seafood can be separately pan-fried or steamed then
stirred through. If you prefer a mushroom risotto,
replace the pumpkin with 2 cups of sliced mushrooms.*

What went wrong

- Using long grain rice. You must use Arborio to get the lovely creamy texture.
- Washing the rice—never, ever, ever!
- Not cooking the base ingredients—there will be no 'base' flavour to get it all started!
- Too many ingredients! My favourite type of risotto is lovely and simple with just one flavour.
- Not boiling the stock.
- Make sure you don't undercook the grain. It should be plump with a little bit of bite and texture.
- Serving the risotto dry and stodgy. It should be soft and oozy and thick and luscious.

METHOD

Use risotto rice (eg arborio, carnaroli).

Place the stock and wine into a saucepan bring to the boil and have simmering away. If it evaporates off and you find you need another ½ cup liquid or so, have a boiled kettle close by and top up when needed.

Melt the butter and oil in a BIG and heavy-based saucepan until foamy. Cook the onion and celery over a medium low heat until soft. Add the vegetables and cook, stirring until lightly golden.

Add the rice and stir through, coating in butter and oil.

Pour in the wine and stir well, then start adding 1 cup (or 1 ladle) of HOT stock at a time stirring. When the liquid has been absorbed add the next ladleful. Keep the hot stock lightly simmering away.

When all the stock is added the rice should be looking plump and cooked, but not overcooked, so taste a little. If it seems not cooked, keep stirring, adding a little extra boiling water (½ cup should do it). It will take around 20 minutes to add the stock ladle by ladle, and by then the risotto will be just about done.

Stir in the remaining butter or cream and the parmesan cheese.

Serve immediately with fresh herbs and extra parmesan.

Fabulous when there seems 'little' in the fridge—a handful of ingredients and dinner is on the table.

Steamed Rice

Serves 2–4

EQUIPMENT
large bowl, fine colander or sieve (optional), heavy-based saucepan with a tight-fitting lid, liquid and cup measurements, scales, fork for fluffing

INGREDIENTS
1 cup long rain rice (jasmine, basmati, etc)
cold water (test using the knuckle method, see below) OR 1 cup rice to 1½ cups water or vegetable or chicken stock
salt (if desired)
30g (1oz) knob butter, to serve
good squeeze lemon juice, to serve
butter, herbs, lemon juice and seasoning, to serve if desired.

Recipe can be halved or doubled if desired.

METHOD
Wash the raw rice in cold water, gently swirling it with your hand. Tip off the water and repeat a couple of times until the water runs clearer. You can use a sieve or colander if you wish and run the cold water tap over it, but choose a fine colander or you will lose lots of the rice.

Place the washed rice into a heavy-based saucepan. Cover with cold water until the water reaches the first knuckle of your index finger when it is placed on the rice. I was taught this method as a very young girl, and it has never let me down! Try it … somehow it works. Or use 1 cup of rice to about 1½ cups water.

Cover with a lid and bring to the boil. The lid will jiggle and you will nearly have water overflowing. Turn down to a very low heat. Cook about 15–20 minutes. (Don't be tempted to peak or you will allow all the lovely steam to drift out of the pot.)

Remove the lid and fluff up the rice with a fork. Season as desired with your favourite things, like butter, lemon juice and salt to taste.

What went wrong

- Using the wrong rice! Long grain is best for steaming so use a basmati or jasmine.
- Not washing the rice before cooking. This will remove the excess starch and result in fluffier rice.
- Not measuring the water—either in cups or with the knuckle technique. Too much and rice will fall apart. Too little and rice will be undercooked.
- Overcooking, so it's soggy or undercooking, so it's crunchy

Meat & Fish

A Perfect Steak

Serves 4

EQUIPMENT

chopping board, sharp knife, heavy-based frying pan, barbecue plate or char-grill pan, tongs, plate for standing, sheet of foil

. . . .

INGREDIENTS

4 x 2–2.5cm (about 1in) thick steaks, such as Sirloin, Porterhouse or Scotch fillet
4 tablespoons olive oil
sea salt and freshly ground black pepper

A good steak looks good before it's even cooked. Rich red, bright colour with marbling. My favourite is sirloin or porterhouse ... or for a little more chew, choose rump. For super tenderness go for an eye fillet. The same cooking rules apply.

METHOD

Buy good steak. The best you can afford (it's important to have the best starting point).

Remove the steaks from any plastic bag and place onto a paper towel-lined plate. Lightly cover and refrigerate until needed.

Remove the steak from the refrigerator about 20 minutes before cooking

If you want to trim off any scraggly bits or the fat (this I definitely do not do myself) use a sharp knife and trim carefully (fat is flavour remember).

Rub the steaks generously with the oil and season well with salt and pepper.

Heat the grill plate, barbecue or pan over a medium high heat until hot.

Add the steaks and allow to cook (and sizzle) for at least 3 minutes before moving. (You want to build up a golden brown crust!) If the pan seems too hot, reduce the temperature a little (but only a little), but keep it hot.

Turn the steaks over gently with the tongs. Many say only twice yet I have learnt much from celebrated meat chefs who claim at least five turns, so I like to split the difference and do three!

Cooking times: Rare: about 3 minutes each side; medium about 4 minutes each and well done about 5 minutes each side.

OR test with a meat thermometer, inserting it gently into the centre of the thickest section of the steak: 35°C (95°F): rare, 65°C (150°F): medium, 75°C (165°F): well done

Standing time is VITAL. Remove steaks and set aside for at least 5 minutes loosely covered with a sheet of foil.

What went wrong

- Remove the meat from any plastic and place on a paper-lined plate, lightly cover and refrigerate until cooking.
- Don't cook cold steak: remove the steak from the refrigerator at least 15 minutes before cooking.
- Rub the steak with oil, don't oil the grill or pan—this splatters, causes flame-ups.
- Heat the char-grill, barbecue plate or heavy-based frying pan. Don't cook steak in a cold pan! This will cause stewing and make it tough.
- Over-turning, poking and playing with the meat. Treat it gently with love!
- Cutting the steak to see if its cooked. Use a thermometer or understand how the meat looks and feels to estimate its level of cooking.

A Succulent Pork Chop

Serves 4

EQUIPMENT

chopping board, sharp knife, griddle pan or heavy-based frying pan,
  tongs, meat thermometer (if you have one), plate for standing

INGREDIENTS

4 x thick-cut pork loin chops or trimmed (Frenched) pork cutlets or pork
  steak (about 2cm (¾in) thick)
about 3 tablespoons olive oil
sea salt and freshly ground black pepper
2 tablespoons chicken stock or white wine
fresh chopped thyme or rosemary

METHOD

Chat to your butcher about the best choice (if wanting pork cutlets ask
the butcher to trim them for you 'French style').

Remove the pork from any plastic and place on a paper towel-lined
plate and loosely cover, refrigerate until needed.

Remove chops from the fridge and let set aside for 10 minutes. Lightly
smear with the olive oil and season with salt and pepper.

Heat barbecue plate, griddle pan or frying pan until hot over a medium
high heat.

Add the pork and cook for 3–4 minutes on each side. Turn two or three
times during the cooking. Don't overcook the pork. A little pink in the
centre is a good thing. Pork should be succulent and tender.

Using a thermometer, pierce into the thickest part of the chop. You
need a reading around 65°C (150°F) to 70°C (160°F). Remove the chops
from the pan and place on a plate to stand—allow meat to stand for at
least 5 minutes please, lightly cover with foil if you like.

What went wrong

- Over-fatty cheap pork!
- Male pork—only ever buy female pork and the
  best you can get (get to know your butcher so
  you can chat about these kinds of things).
- Overcooking, so easily done with pork, and
  DON'T believe those silly old fashioned
  stories about pork needing to be well cooked!
- Too thin—choose chops that are at least
  15cm (6in) thick. If the meat is more than
  2cm (about an inch) thick, you are best to
  sear them on each side in a hot pan (see
  A Perfect Steak recipe). and then cook in a
  180°C (350°F) oven for around 5 minutes or
  check with a thermometer if not sure.
- Grilling/broiling! I'm not so keen on cooking
  under a grill, the meat tends to shrink and
  shrivel.

Plump Lamb Chops

Serves 4

EQUIPMENT

chopping board, sharp knife, fine grater, small bowl, griddle pan, barbecue plate or heavy-based fry pan

. . . .

INGREDIENTS

8 (at least) lamb chops (you can ask the butcher to cut them thicker, even up to a double chop, which is about 4.5cm thick, if you like)

2 tablespoons olive oil

finely grated rind and juice 1 lemon

2 cloves garlic, finely chopped

sea salt and freshly ground black pepper

couple sprigs fresh rosemary, leaves stripped and roughly chopped (optional)

Gorgeous, thick, delicious ... so good.

What went wrong

- Old lamb—buy the best and sweetest smelling. You need a good butcher!
- Skinny, uneven, scraggly looking. I like thick-cut chops all of a similar size.
- Chops cooked at a heat that's too high so they burn and lose the succulence they should have. Juicy is what we want.
- Turning and turning and turning, poking and prodding. This makes the meat tough. Leave your meat alone!

METHOD

Choose evenly sized chops.

Combine the oil, lemon rind, a good pinch of sea salt and plenty of freshly ground pepper. Use your hands to rub the mixture all over the chops. If time allows, refrigerate in a sealed container and allow to marinate overnight.

Heat a griddle pan, barbecue plate or couple of large frying pans over a medium heat. When hot, place on the chops. Cook for a few minutes before turning. (I turn thick chops regularly so they cook evenly.)

Cook about 7–10 minutes or until cooked to your liking. (During the cooking I like to drizzle over small splashes of lemon juice … not too much. I find it adds moisture and a delicious lemon flavour.)

You can test them with a meat thermometer in the thickest part of the chop. Medium is about 70°C (160°F).

Serve with your favourite salad or vegetables.

Tip: Don't add too much lemon juice at a time or you will drown the chops and force them to stew … just add a little spritz at a time. If cooking with double or thick chops you must use a meat thermometer and allow at least 10 minutes of standing time before serving.

Sensational Sausages

Serves 4

EQUIPMENT

chopping board, scissors, large saucepan, tongs, colander, paper towel, frying pan

INGREDIENTS

8 good-quality large sausages (any flavour you like) just good quality (a coarse texture is always nice), from a good butcher
2 tablespoons olive oil
mustard or tomato sauce

METHOD

Once home remove the sausages from any plastic bag and place on a paper towel-lined plate, lightly cover and refrigerate until needed

Place the sausages on the chopping board and, if connected together in links, carefully separate into individual sausages using the scissors

Place the sausages in a large saucepan and cover with cold water. Place over a medium heat and bring up to a gentle boil. Simmer 1 minute.

Drain into a colander and pat dry.

Drizzle the olive oil over the sausages and toss well to coat. Heat a barbecue plate, char-grill pan or frying pan over a medium heat.

When hot add the sausages and cook 4–5 minutes turning often until golden brown and cooked. Serve with mash or salad and crusty bread if desired.

Alternatively, fry the lightly oiled sausages until just golden. Then transfer to a 180°C (350°F)/160°C (320°F) fan-forced oven and cook about 15 minutes. This ensures the sausages are browned, plump and cooked through, but doesn't remove any of the fat!

What went wrong

- Pricking and poking them. This only makes them split and explode. All the lovely juices will come out leaving your pan burnt and greasy and your sausages dry!
- Cooking over a too-high heat so burnt on the outside and not cooked through!
- Greasy fatty texture? Cheap nasty sausages—always, always buy the best you can.

Roast Lamb

Serves 4

EQUIPMENT

chopping board, small sharp knife, large cook's knife, fine grater, trivet or rack, baking dish, large sheets foil

· ·

INGREDIENTS

1.5kg (3lb 5oz) small leg lamb

4 cloves garlic, peeled and cut into long slivers

3 stalks fresh rosemary (or lemon thyme is delicious too), removed from the stalk and chopped

finely grated zest and juice 1 large lemon (choose a nice juicy one)

50ml (1¾fl oz) olive oil

sea salt flakes and freshly ground black pepper

2 tablespoons honey or maple syrup (optional)

QUICK GRAVY

125ml (4fl oz) white wine (something you would drink)

500ml (17½fl oz) chicken stock (if using stock cubes, choose low salt—as cubes can be salty)

2 tablespoons tomato puree

1–2 tablespoons red currant jelly (or plum jam will do, add just enough, not too sweet)

freshly ground black pepper

Surely this is a signature dish? Do it well and you've mastered a classic!

METHOD

Buy good lamb—it should be firm, pink and a nice plump-looking leg/ Leave on a little fat too: it adds to the flavour.

Once home, remove from any plastic or packaging. Wipe with paper towel and place on a paper towel-lined plate. Refrigerate until ready to prepare.

Remove lamb from the refrigerator about 15 minutes before cooking. Don't cook the lamb cold; bringing it near room temperature improves the flavour and texture of the roast.

Preheat the oven to 180°C (350°F)/160°F (320°F) fan-forced and put a small rack or trivet into the base of your baking dish.

Cut several small slits over the lamb. Push a slither of garlic into each slit. Combine the herbs with the lemon zest, juice, oil and salt and pepper. Rub this herby lemon mixture over the lamb.

Roast 15 minutes per 500g (17½oz) (for 1.5kg/53oz leg this is 45 minutes) Drizzle with the honey or maple syrup then remove the lamb and wrap in the foil.

Stand set aside for 15 minutes. No skipping this step as standing is the big secret to the tenderness and succulence.

Thinly slice the lamb and serve with your favourite vegetables, and the gravy of course.

GRAVY

While the meat is standing, remove the trivet/rack from the baking dish. Tip off the excess oil (you just need the yummy juices). Place the baking dish onto the stove and bring juices to the boil, stirring regularly. Add the wine (there will be lots of bubbling here) and then the chicken stock, keep stirring. Add the red currant jelly and season with salt and pepper. Stir over a high heat incorporating any caramelised yummy bits from the bottom or sides of the dish. Simmer and bubble away for about 5 minutes until you have about 1½ cups gravy. Check the juices from the lamb—there will be some pooled in the foil—tip this flavoursome liquid into the gravy.

What went wrong

- Not knowing the weight of the lamb leg—the rule of thumb for roasting lamb to medium is 15 minutes per 500g (18oz), so know the weight to cook beautiful lamb.
- Roasting in a too-high heat. Keep it moderate 180°C/350°F is perfect so that the meat cooks slowly.
- Cooking cold straight from the fridge. Remove the lamb from the fridge for at least 15 minutes before cooking to help bring it towards room temperature for even cooking.
- Placing straight in the baking dish—the lamb will stew in its own juices, so place on a rack in side the dish.
- Lack of seasoning, herbs or oil, which will make the roast dull and uninteresting flavour.
- Not standing before carving or serving—allow to stand at least 15 minutes in a warm spot or wrap the leg in a large sheet of foil. This lets the juices settle in the meat, instead of draining out when you cut it.

Bolognese Sauce

Serves 4–6

EQUIPMENT

scales, chopping board, sharp knife, large, deep heavy-based
    pan with lid, slotted spoon, large wooden spoon, spatula,
    fork, liquid measuring jug

. . . .

INGREDIENTS

3 tablespoons olive oil

40g (1½oz) butter

4 cloves garlic, finely chopped

1 stick celery, finely diced

1 large brown onion, finely diced

2 small carrots, finely chopped

500g (17½oz) good-quality beef mince (or the same quantity
    diced blade or rump and mince it yourself or ask the butcher)

400g (14oz) pork mince (or the same quantity of diced pork
    from the leg, mince it yourself or ask the butcher)

2 more tablespoons olive oil (if needed)

6 rashers good bacon (something smoky or you can use
    150g (5oz) chopped salami)

1 big fat anchovy, well-mashed (optional)

250ml (9fl oz) red wine

250ml (9fl oz) beef stock (I always buy salt reduced)

2 x 420g (15oz) cans chopped tomatoes (choose a brand
    that has plump, red, good quality tomatoes, often they are
    the cheapest Italian brand)

1 litre (36fl oz) passata sauce (again a good, cheap Italian
    brand)

2 bay leaves or 2 sprigs thyme

½ cup chopped fresh parsley (I love this stirred through
    towards the end of the simmering)

plenty of sea salt and freshly ground black pepper

your favourite pasta (mine is thick parpadelle or a ribbed
    rigatoni), to serve

METHOD

Heat the oil and butter in a big, large, deep pan (preferably with a heavy base). Add the garlic, onion, celery and carrot. Cook over a medium heat, stirring, for 5 minutes or until softened (and looking glossy). Remove from the pan with a slotted spoon and set aside.

Reheat the pan, add about half of the beef and pork mince and stir well. Using a fork or wooden spoon break up the lumps (kind of pushing the mince into the pan). If the pan gets too full, remove the browned mince before reheating the pan and adding more. If you need a little more oil add it, but make sure the pan is hot before adding the mince (or it will stew in the oil).

Add the remaining mince and brown (squashing out the lumps).

Return all of the browned meat, softened vegetables, bacon and anchovy to the pan. Bring to the boil. Stir in the red wine and cook 2 minutes. Add the stock, tomatoes, tomato sauce and bay leaves or thyme and season well with the salt and pepper. Bring to a gentle boil, then reduce the heat to low. Partially cover (this is about ¾ over the top of the pan with the lid) and simmer gently for at least 1½ hours (if you have time, 2 hours is even better).

Pop back every 20 minutes or so and have a stir. Keep the heat low and just let it gently bubble away. About 15 minutes before serving, stir in the freshly chopped parsley

Serve with your favourite pasta and freshly grated, good-flavoured parmesan cheese

To cook the pasta: Bring the largest saucepan you have to the boil with salted water. When really boiling add the pasta and stir. Let it come back to the boil then cook for about 8 minutes (but don't cover the pan or it will boil over). Grab a bit of the pasta and taste it—it should be just tender: please don't overcook it. Drain the pasta quickly, leaving some water on it. This will help it toss well with the sauce. Return the pasta to the saucepan and keep it warm until ready to serve.

What went wrong

- Fatty 'chunky' mince (buy the best you can afford). Yes it can have some marbling but not solid fat and I like to buy the meat and mince it myself or ask the butcher to mince it ... some mince has terrible preservatives and additives added to it.
- Don't use just beef: pork mince adds a marvellous flavour. True Bolognese recipes are often made with pork mince—not beef.
- Burnt onion or garlic (yuk the flavour will ruin the sauce).
- Under-seasoned—be sure to taste and use a good amount of salt and pepper and remember the herbs are important.
- Under-simmered (simmer for at least 1 and a half hours). If you don't simmer the bolognese for long enough, the sauce will not have absorbed into the meat enough to meld flavours and textures and the meat may remain in lumps from the browning process.

Fab Roast Chicken

Serves 4–6

EQUIPMENT

chopping board, sharp knife or scissors, kitchen string, large roasting pan with rack, sheet of foil to cover

. . . .

INGREDIENTS

1 large, size 18, free-range chicken (organic if possible)
3 lemons
several sprigs lemon thyme
100ml (3½fl oz) olive oil
sea salt and freshly ground black pepper
2 heads garlic

A favourite that for me is definitely in the 'last meal' category. Good chicken is a must, I cook a roast chicken every week. I hope you love this version.

METHOD

Buy the freshest, best quality chicken you can afford, free-range and/or organic

Remove the chicken from any plastic. Remove the neck and large pieces of fat from the neck. Rinse the chicken well under cold water and drain. Pat dry inside and out with paper towel. Place on a paper towel-lined plate, lightly cover and refrigerate.

For amazing crispy skin: pour boiling water over the chicken. You will see the skin plump up. Pat dry with paper towel.

Preheat the oven to 200°C (400°F). Place a rack inside a large baking dish.

Cut the lemons in half, place two halves inside the chicken with a couple of sprigs of thyme. Tuck the wings underneath and trim off the bottom section of the wing, if you like, using scissors. Tie the legs together firmly with kitchen string.

Rub the chicken all over with olive oil, using your hands. Sprinkle well with salt and pepper.

Place the chicken breast-side up onto the rack in the roasting pan. Cut the garlic heads through the centre, drizzle with a little oil and pop into the roasting pan along with the remaining lemon halves.

Roast for 1 hour then baste (just spoon over) with some of the juices and oil from the bottom of the pan. Roast a further 30–40 minutes. Test the chicken with the tip of a knife into the thickest section of the thigh. The juices should run clear.

Remove the chicken and set aside to rest, covering lightly with a sheet of foil.

The chicken is delicious served with gravy (see page 137) and any of the vegetable sides (see the 'Vegetables' chapter of this book, especially roast potatoes and honey carrots.

What went wrong

- Not rinsing inside and out or patting dry the chicken before roasting: rinsing and drying makes crispy skin.
- Not placing chicken on a rack means that the chicken will stew in its juices rather than roast.
- Not tucking in the wings or trussing and tying the legs together (the chicken will cook unevenly and get burnt and dried out on the wings and legs).
- Lack of seasoning and too-low temperature encourages stewing and lack of moisture.
- Undercooking or overcooking! Undercooking chicken can be dangerous—juices should run clear in the thickest part of the thigh and meat should be cooked through. Overcooking can mean dry flavourless meat!

Spice-crusted Chicken

Serves 4

EQUIPMENT

chopping board, sharp knife, fine grater, small bowl, spoon, char-grill pan or heavy-based frying pan, tongs, lid to pan

INGREDIENTS

4 large chicken thigh fillets

3 tablespoons olive oil

3 teaspoons ground cumin and coriander

2 teaspoons turmeric

1 teaspoon sea salt and freshly ground black pepper

finely grated rind and juice 2 limes

1 red and 1 green capsicum (bell peppers), cut into strips (to serve if desired)

METHOD

Trim the excess fat from the chicken.

Combine the oil, spices, salt and pepper, and lime rind and smear all over the chicken. If time allows refrigerate and marinate for 1 hour.

Heat the grill over a medium high heat. Place the chicken on the hot grill, cook about 3 minutes then drizzle with a little of the lime juice.

Turn the chicken over and cook 1 minute. Pour over the remaining lime juice and partially cover with the lid. Reduce the heat and cook 2 minutes or until chicken is cooked.

Remove chicken and stand 3 minutes, while tossing the capsicums in the pan or on the grill until just softened.

Pile the capsicum (if using) onto the serving plates, top with the chicken. Serve.

Tip: Test the chicken is cooked by piecing in the thickest part of the thigh fillet with the tip of a knife: the juices will run clear if it is cooked.

What went wrong

- Don't overturn or overcook as the chicken will burn and dry out and will not form the gorgeous golden crust (turn only once or twice during the cooking).
- Cooking wet chicken—always dry with paper towel before smearing with the spice mixture—no shortcuts here please.
- Heat the pan before adding the chicken. If it's too cool the chicken will stew, not sear. You must hear a sizzle.
- Don't add oil to the pan. Smear the chicken with the oil and spice mixture. Adding oil to the pan, causes spitting and mess!

Thai Green Curry

Serves 4

EQUIPMENT

*chopping board, sharp knife, large deep pan or wok,
    wooden spoon or silicon spatula, can opener, ladle or deep
    serving spoon*

. . . .

INGREDIENTS

1 tablespoon sunflower or peanut oil

1 large onion, finely chopped

4cm (1½in) fresh ginger, finely chopped (optional)

3 tablespoons fresh Thai green curry paste*

400ml (14fl oz) coconut milk

250ml (9fl oz) chicken stock

4 Kaffir lime leaves, torn

500g (17½oz) chicken thigh fillet, diced into large pieces

1 tablespoon fish sauce

1 tablespoon grated palm sugar or brown sugar

1 red capsicum (bell pepper), finely sliced

1 cup green beans (tops removed but leave on the tails)

juice from 1 lime

½ bunch coriander fresh leaves

We all need one of these homestyle Thai
curries in our repertoire. So easily made,
just always have a half-good Thai curry
paste in the pantry.

METHOD

Remove the chicken from any plastic or bag, place on a paper towel-lined plate, lightly cover and refrigerate until needed.

Measure and weigh all ingredients before cooking.

Heat the oil over a medium heat. Add the onion, ginger and curry paste and cook, stirring, for 3 minutes or until fragrant DO NOT BURN!

Add the coconut milk, stock and lime leaves. Stirring, bring to the boil then reduce the heat and simmer uncovered for 5 minutes.

Add the chicken and gently poach allowing to just bubble along (do not boil), stirring occasionally for about 4 minutes or until the chicken is cooked.

Add the beans and capsicum and cook for another minute or two.

Add the fish sauce, palm sugar and lime juice.

Spoon into serving bowls, top with coriander and serve with steamed Jasmine rice. Use leftover curry paste within five days or freeze in small tablespoon amount well sealed for up to three months.

Tip: Palm sugar and Thai curry pastes are available from Asian food stores or the Asian section of supermarkets.

What went wrong

- Cutting the chicken into unrecognisable or uneven pieces. This will mean the chicken cooks unevenly.
- Lack of colour and texture in the vegetables in the curry caused by overcooking.
- Split sauce from boiling or cooking over high heat for a long period of time.
- Burning the onion or curry paste this makes a bitter curry. There are two ways to make a Thai curry you can either cook the onion and curry paste in oil until fragrant OR heat the coconut milk and add the curry and poach it. The most common is to cook the paste—but don't burn it.
- Lack of seasoning and flavour balance—you can't see this but oh you will taste it!
- Fake colour—a Thai green curry uses a green chilli base, but it should never glow at you!
- Don't brown the meat. The most popular style for this dish is to simmer the sauce then add the chicken to poach.
- Use chicken thigh fillet to retain succulence and flavour; breast fillets will dry out far too easily.

Chicken Cacciatore

Serves 4

EQUIPMENT

chopping board and sharp knife, paper towel, large heavy-based deep frying pan or braising pan with a lid, silicon spatula or wooden spoon, tongs.

. . . .

INGREDIENTS

4 chicken marylands (this is the leg with the thigh attached or you can use chicken thighs if preferred)

2 tablespoons olive oil

1 onion, cut into large chunks

1 carrot, cut into large chunks

1 stick celery, thickly sliced

½ red capsicum (bell pepper), cut into rough pieces

3 sprigs fresh oregano, chopped

1 anchovy, finely chopped (a must: don't worry you won't taste it but it adds a sensational base flavour)

⅔ cup tomato paste

2 tablespoons orange juice

125ml (4fl oz/about ½ cup) red wine

½ cup pitted Kalamata olives

freshly ground salt and black pepper

1 punnet cherry tomatoes

A great standby for gatherings or family meals. The flavour should be rich but with a slight softness and sweetness. I like to add cherry tomatoes just before serving.

What went wrong

- Using the wrong chicken cut—I like a Maryland (this is the leg with the thigh attached, or use either one separately). You need a succulent cut like the thigh or the leg as the breast is too dry!
- Browning the chicken over a too-cool temperature means the pieces will soak in the oil.
- Cutting the vegetables too small so they mash into the sauce. What's the point? You want to taste and feel them in the dish.
- Underseasoning so the chicken is flavourless—use good quality fresh chicken!
- Boiling vigorously so the sauce separates and oil rises to the surface.
- Boiling and overcooking the chicken so it becomes dry and tough.

METHOD

Once home remove the chicken from any plastic or bag. Place on a paper towel-lined plate and lightly cover, refrigerate until needed.

Pat the chicken pieces dry with paper towel.

Rub the chicken all over with some of the oil. Heat a large, heavy-based pan over a medium heat.

Add the remaining oil, with the onion, carrot and celery. Cook, tossing, for about 8 minutes or until golden, stirring often. DO NOT burn. Remove from the pan.

Add the chicken and brown well on all sides. Return the onion mixture and the capsicum, oregano and anchovy. Stir in the tomato paste, orange juice and wine then bring the mixture to the boil.

Place in a moderate oven and cook 40 minutes or simmer partially covered over a low heat or 20 minutes or until chicken is tender. Do not boil.

Stir in the olives and cherry tomatoes and season to taste with the salt and pepper. Simmer until the tomatoes just soften.

Crumbed Schnitzel

Serves 4

EQUIPMENT

chopping board, sharp knife, rolling pin, hand whisk or fork, 3 x wide yet shallow bowls like soup bowls, food processor with all-purpose chopping blade, large frying pan, tongs, paper towel or a cooling rack

. . . .

INGREDIENTS

4 medium-sized chicken breast fillets (about 180g/6oz each)
4 slices day-old wholemeal or white bread
½ cup plain (all-purpose) flour (or fine rice flour)
3 eggs whisked with 2 tablespoons water
pinch sea salt and freshly ground black pepper
vegetable oil for shallow frying (about 750ml/24fl oz)

This recipe can be halved or doubled if desired.

Schnitzels are a great quick meal. Normally fried, this method for cooking is called shallow frying. The oil needs to come about halfway up the chicken, pork or veal steak. The schnitzel is turned over halfway through the cooking.

METHOD

Trim and separate the tenderloin (the long thin piece of chicken underneath) from the fillet. This can be crumbed and cooked separately or use in a stir-fry.

Using the rolling pin, pat out the fillet, without tearing, to an even thickness of around 1.5cm (¾in).

Place the bread into a food processor and finely chop to smooth breadcrumbs (I like to leave the crusts on the bread for some texture).

Place the crumbs into one of the bowls, and the flour, with salt and pepper, into another.

Whisk the eggs and water together with the small whisk and place in remaining bowl. You will now have three separate bowls with mixtures: flour, egg mixture and breadcrumbs.

Using one hand only, lightly coat each breast fillet in flour, shaking off any additional flour. Then coat in the egg mixture. Using your other, clean, hand, coat each fillet in the breadcrumbs, lightly pressing the crumbs on. Repeat with the remaining chicken fillets and tenderloin sections (if using).

Refrigerate for 30 minutes (this helps the crumbing stay on).

Fill a large deep frying pan about ⅓ way with oil and heat to 180°C (350°F)—sprinkle a few breadcrumbs into the oil: they will sizzle and colour within 5 seconds when the oil is ready, or use a thermometer to test (these are available from cookware stores).

Carefully place the chicken fillets into the hot oil. If the pan is too full, cook the chicken in two batches. Cook about 3 minutes or until lightly golden, carefully turn over with tongs and cook the other side for 3 minutes.

Remove from the oil and drain on paper towel or a rack. Serve immediately.

Variation: Pork loin steaks or veal steaks or boneless chicken thigh fillets can be used. Be sure to pat out the meat as above so it is even in thickness.

What went wrong

- Meat or chicken too thick or uneven (the schnitzel will cook unevenly).
- Crumbing unevenly coated or too thick and gluggy.
- The oil not hot enough (the schnitzel absorbs oil and the crumb will fall off).
- Frying pan over-crowded—this reduces the temperature of the oil and causes the schnitzel to get soggy.
- Not draining correctly by placing cooked schnitzel on crumpled paper towel or a cooling rack. Place it on paper towel. This is the best way of getting rid of excess oil.

Pan-fried Fish Fillets

Serves 4

EQUIPMENT

paper towel, plate or chopping board, shape knife, heavy-based frying pan, two egg slides

· ·

INGREDIENTS

4 FRESH fillets of firm white fish
sea salt flakes
freshly ground black pepper
3 tablespoons olive oil
small 10g (¹/₃oz) knob butter (if desired)
fresh chopped parley, chives and or sprig thyme (if desired)
lemon wedges

This recipe can be halved or doubled if desired.

Tip: How to tell if fish is cooked: The flesh turns very white and, using a fork or tip of a knife, gently flake the fish at the thickest part, the flesh will easily flake. Most people tend to overcook fish. The fish will continue to cook once removed from the pan. It is best to have the other items, such as tossed salad, almost ready before adding the fish. With fish, timing is everything.

Make sure the fish is FRESH, super fresh, and pat dry with paper towel before cooking. It's really as simple as seasoning lightly, cooking simply and serving immediately.

METHOD

Buy FRESH fish! Chat to the fishmonger and ask what is best on the day. If buying 'frozen', defrost before cooking.

Once home, remove fish from the bag and place on a sheet of paper towel on a plate. Lightly cover with extra paper towel or plastic wrap and refrigerate until cooking. ALWAYS cook on the day purchased!

Remove fish from the refrigerator and pat dry with some extra paper towel. Trim any skinny ends and or even up the fillet. Skinny ends will overcook and toughen drying out. If the fillet is quite thick, cut a couple of slashes into the thickest section with a sharp knife. This allows the fish to cook evenly.

Heat a heavy-based frying pan over a medium high heat until hot: lightly smear the fish on both sides with the olive oil. (I like to oil the fish itself not place oil in the pan as I find this splashes and spits when the fish is added.)

Run your hand over the top of the pan and when it feels hot then add the fish carefully. Depending on the size of the pan you should be able to add four fillets, but if the pan looks overcrowded, cook in two separate batches, reheating the pan in between and placing the batch cooked first on a plate in a 150°C/300°F oven, while you cook the second batch OR do as I do and use two separate pans at once!

Cook the fish quite quickly for about 2 minutes (this depends on the thickness of the fillet). Turn over carefully using two egg slides so as to not break the fillet. (I find it best not to use tongs when cooking fish.) If adding butter, add it to the hot pan now. The butter will quickly melt into the olive oil juices in the pan. Cook about 1 minute further before removing

Sprinkle with freshly chopped herbs (if using) and a squeeze of lemon juice and serve immediately

What went wrong

- Fish that is NOT fresh. Always buy fresh for the best flavour.
- Buying the wrong fish—too thin for pan frying will mean it will dry out and overcook quickly—ask your fishmonger if unsure.
- Cooking fish in a cold pan. If the pan is not hot enough to colour and sear it will stew in its own juices.
- Over-turning or poking during cooking—leave him alone when he's cooking.
- Overcooking—dry, dry, dry.

Crispy Deep-fried Fish

Serves 4

EQUIPMENT

scales or cup measures, liquid measuring jug, standmixer with whisk attachment, larger, deep, high-sided saucepan, wok or deep fryer, plate for flour, thermometer, tongs, paper towel

INGREDIENTS

BATTER

½ cup (68g) plain (all-purpose) flour
½ cup (80g) potato flour or cornflour
3 teaspoons baking powder
1 teaspoon salt
1 egg yolk
200ml (7fl oz) cold water

OTHER

2 litres (70fl oz) vegetable oil
500g (17½oz) your favourite boneless fish fillets
1 cup plain (all-purpose) flour, extra
sea salt, to serve
lemon wedges, to serve

Hard to resist golden-brown, crispy deep fried fish ... for me, make it flat-head tails or deep-sea perch please.

What went wrong

- Fish that is too thickly coated in batter will never get crispy on the outside and cooked all the way through.
- Overmixed batter, which makes it tough.
- Oil not the correct frying temperature. If the oil is too cold the batter will not go a golden deep-fried colour and will soak up the oil, making the fish greasy and oily.
- Fish not floured before battering—the batter will fall off.
- Batter too thick or oil too hot? The batter will be overcooked on outside and gooey and uncooked on the inside.

METHOD

Weigh and measure all ingredients carefully.

Place the batter ingredients into the bowl of your standmixer with the beater attachment and mix on speed 2 (or low) until just combined. (Or use a mixing bowl and a wooden spoon to mix batter ingredients together quickly to a just smooth consistency.) Don't overmix.

Dry fish fillets with paper towel, and lightly coat in extra flour.

Heat oil in a large, deep saucepan, wok or deep-fryer over a medium heat to 180°C (350°F) (only ever fill the pan to half full with oil). Test with a thermometer or drop a few crumbs bread into the hot oil. The bread will lightly sizzle and brown when the oil is hot enough—remove from the oil. Dip and coat the fish in batter. Allow excess batter to drain off then place gently into the oil. Do not over crowd the pan. Cook 2 pieces at once only

Cook 2–3 minutes until golden. Using tongs gently remove fish from the oil. Drain lightly on paper towel. Serve immediately.

Tip: Lightly coating the fish in flour before the batter helps the batter adhere to the fish and not fall off. For extra crispy batter try using cold soda water instead of tap water.

Barbecue Salmon Steaks

Serves 4

EQUIPMENT

chopping board, sharp knife, fine grater, small bowl, spoon, clean char-grill plate or barbecue plate, tongs, 2 egg slides

. . . .

INGREDIENTS

4 x 200g (7oz) salmon steaks, skin on
3 tablespoons olive oil
freshly grated rind of 2 medium lemons
good pinch sea salt
3 sprigs fresh thyme (leaves picked)
freshly ground black pepper

This recipe can be halved or doubled if desired.

Barbecue salmon steaks or cutlets have to be one of the easiest and most delicious meals. The secret is in the cooking—don't dry out that salmon: leave it nice and pink in the centre. Marinating can be quickly done before cooking if desired. I like to serve with cucumber ribbons and a little dill—it's so very clean tasting.

METHOD

Remove the salmon from the fridge, trim off any skinny scraggly pieces with a sharp knife and discard.

Combine the oil with the thyme, lemon rind, salt and pepper in a small bowl. Smear all over the salmon.

Heat a clean char-grill plate or barbecue plate over a medium high heat until smoking slightly. Place the salmon, skin side down, onto the grill and don't move it! Cook until the skin is crispy and browned (about 3 minutes only).

Carefully using two egg slides, turn the steaks over and cook the other side for a further 2–3 minutes (be careful and don't be tempted to overcook).

Remove and serve immediately.

What went wrong

- Using a dirty grill plate—CLEAN it! The fish will stick if it's not spotless.
- Using a grill plate that is not hot enough (sticky, sticky, sticky!).
- Too much turning, poking and prodding when cooking (the skin will be damaged and it will break up and fall apart).
- Choose salmon pieces similar in size so they cook evenly.
- Removing the skin. Cook with the skin on please. It crisps up and is delicious and also helps the fish stay moist.
- Incorrect storage. Don't store fish in a plastic bag. Remove salmon from the bag as soon as you're home and place on a paper towel–lined plate. Lightly cover with paper towel or plastic wrap and refrigerate until cooking.
- Too much oil on the plate—it will be soggy and get smoky (I like to smear the fish with oil, not the barbecue plate).
- Don't use tongs or forks to turn your fish. These are too rough and will break the fish.

Vegetables

Crisp Green Beans

Serves 4

EQUIPMENT

medium-sized heavy-based frying pan, wooden spoon or silicon spatula, plate, medium-sized saucepan, colander, fine grater, tongs

INGREDIENTS

50g (1¾oz) pecans, roughly chopped
good pinch sea salt flakes
500g (17½oz) green beans, trimmed
2 tablespoons (40g/1½oz) butter
2 teaspoons finely grated lemon rind or juice (the rind packs more flavour)
freshly ground black pepper

METHOD

Put the pecans into the frying pan. Cook over a medium low heat for 5 minutes, gently stirring regularly until they turn a light golden brown (don't burn them).

Remove from the pan to a plate (they will keep cooking if kept in the pan).

Half-fill the saucepan with water. Cover and bring to the boil. Add salt and the beans and cook for 3–4 minutes (or until they are bright green and tender yet crisp).

Drain into the colander, shaking off the excess water. Put the beans back into the pan.

Return the saucepan to the heat. Add the butter and cover. Cook 2 minutes, shaking the pan gently. Add the lemon, black pepper and pecans. Toss well with the tongs. Serve immediately.

Tip: Pecans can be replaced for almonds if desired.

A great side when beans are in season—crisp, fresh and delish—just don't overcook them.

What went wrong

- Burning the nuts.
- Cooking the beans in too much water—this drowns them.
- Overcooking, making the beans soggy, soggy, soggy, not to mention loss of flavour and nutrients.
- Not draining well—they stay watery.

Honey Carrots

Serves 4

EQUIPMENT

*Chopping board, vegetable peeler, cook's knife, large heavy-based
saucepan with lid, colander, tongs, teaspoon and tablespoon measure*

INGREDIENTS

500g (17½oz) medium-sized carrots (or a large bunch of Dutch carrots)
water to JUST cover
2 tablespoons butter
3 teaspoons of your favourite honey
good pinch salt flakes
freshly ground black pepper

METHOD

Trim the ends from the carrots and peel the skin (if desired). Cut the
carrots in half lengthwise and each half lengthwise (if using Dutch carrots,
you can leave them whole or just cut them in half lengthways and leave a
little green stem on).

   Place into the saucepan and top with just enough water to cover (don't
drown them). Partially cover with a lid and bring to the boil over a medium
heat. Once boiling, cook for 3–4 minutes (about half cooked).

   Drain in a colander and return the carrots to the pan with the butter
and honey. Cook over a medium high heat, tossing occasionally with the
tongs for 3 minutes (you can also give the pan a good shake too). Cook
until the carrots are just tender and very glossy.

   Season well and serve.

*A tried and true favourite! Try with a
combination of carrots and parsnips.*

What went wrong

- Carrots cut too small or unevenly (they will
  all cook to different stages! Some soft, some
  hard).
- Cooking in too much water (carrots will
  become waterlogged, lose flavour and
  colour).
- Overcooking (test with the tip of a knife or
  pierce with a fork).

Cauliflower Cheese

Serves 4

EQUIPMENT

scales and/or measuring cups, liquid measuring jug, medium to large heavy-based saucepan and lid, wooden spoon or silicon spatula, small balloon whisk, course grater, colander, 3 litre (105fl oz) ovenproof baking dish

. . . .

INGREDIENTS

150g (5oz) Cheddar cheese
80g (2½oz) Parmesan cheese
1 large cauliflower
100g (3½oz) butter
½ cup (80g/2½oz) plain (all-purpose) flour (or rice flour for a gluten-free sauce)
1 litre (36fl oz) milk (full cream or low fat)
salt flakes and freshly ground black pepper
good pinch ground nutmeg

This recipe can be halved or doubled if preferred.

A simple but special side dish that comforts the tummy and the soul—just right as part of a roast dinner or next to a great steak.

What went wrong

- Overcooking the cauliflower until it's waterlogged
- Too much cheese, making the dish oily and greasy.
- Overcooked roux in the white sauce with burnt brown bits.
- Not enough whisking or stirring of the sauce (lumps and sauce catches and burns on the base of the pan).
- Flour–butter mixture (the roux) not cooked enough (sauce will taste floury).

METHOD

Grate the cheeses and set aside.

Preheat the oven to 180°C (350°F). Lightly butter a large 3 litre (105fl oz) ovenproof dish.

Fill the saucepan about one-third full with cold water and salt. Cover and bring to the boil.

Meanwhile, trim the base and outside leaves from the cauliflower. Cut into florettes (this is a cluster of the buds on the stem). Trim off excess stalk and slice into thin pieces (I like to eat the stalk too).

Add the cauliflower to the water (the water should just cover the cauliflower). Cover with the lid and cook about 3 minutes only. It will be just beginning to soften.

Drain well into the colander and discard the water. Rinse gently under cold water (this will stop the cauliflower overcooking). Arrange the cauliflower in the buttered dish.

Lightly dry the saucepan. Melt the butter in the saucepan over a medium heat until foamy (do not burn).

Add in the flour and stir constantly for 2 minutes (this mixture is called a roux). Cook until the mixture is a sandy colour (take care not to burn the mixture).

Remove the pan from the heat. Add the milk (all in one go) and whisk in quickly. Put the pan back onto the heat. Bring to the boil over a medium low heat, stirring constantly until the sauce thickens and bubbles appear (this takes about 3 minutes). Don't stop stirring!

Season well with the nutmeg, salt and pepper and stir in about ¾ of the combined cheese. Place back over a low heat and stir until the sauce is smooth and velvety.

Pour the sauce over the cauliflower. Scatter over the remaining cheese. Bake 25 minutes or until lightly golden.

Slow-roasted Tomatoes

EQUIPMENT
heavy-based ovenproof ceramic dish, chopping board, large cook's knife

INGREDIENTS
1.5kg (3lb 5oz) ripe red tomatoes (choose your favourite variety and
preferably vine ripened)
3 cloves garlic, peeled and halved lengthwise
1 fresh chilli, sliced (optional)
1 tablespoon brown sugar
3–4 sprigs fresh thyme or oregano
200ml (7fl oz) olive oil
sea salt flakes and freshly ground black pepper

METHOD
Preheat the oven to 120°C (250°F).

Cut the tomatoes in half and lay them in the dish cut side up. (I like to use a dish the tomatoes fit snuggly into.) Place the garlic and the chilli (If using) in and around the tomatoes and scatter over the herbs.

Pour over the oil and sprinkle a little brown sugar over each of the cut tomatoes. Season well with the salt and pepper.

Roast 1½–2 hours or until the tomatoes have deepened in colour and smell delicious! Allow to cool in the dish.

Use on an antipasti plate or squash onto crunchy thick toast or toss into hot pasta, serve with char-grilled steak, etc. The oil is especially good too!

What went wrong

- Using unripe tomatoes—choose ripe, red well-flavoured or they will never have a delicious, sweet flavour.
- Cooking at too high a temperature—the tomatoes will overcook and stew.
- Lack of sweetness and flavour—add a touch of brown sugar and fresh herbs.
- Only use olive oil (definitely not other styles of oil).
- Lack of seasoning—tomatoes love a good pinch of salt and some pepper!

Sauces

Old-fashioned Gravy

Serves 4

EQUIPMENT

roasting pan from a roast (with the juices), wooden spoon or good quality silicon spatula, small hand whisk, jug for liquid, spoon for tasting

INGREDIENTS

pan juices from roasted meat, about 2 tablespoons
about 1 tablespoon plain (all-purpose) flour*
around 500ml (17½fl oz) well-flavoured beef stock (pre-made in a tetra pack, homemade or good-quality beef stock cube)
about ¼ cup red wine
1 tablespoon red currant jelly or plum jam

METHOD

Drain off the excess oil, but leave good pan juices and all the crispy bits.

Heat over a low heat, and sprinkle in the flour. Using a wooden spoon, stir and incorporate all the bits in the pan, stirring right into the corners. Cook gently, stirring for about 10 minutes OR pop the pan back into the oven and cook 8 minutes or until mixture is brown. If cooking on the stove top, keep stirring and don't allow mixture to burn (it will become bitter).

Add some of the stock and stir well. Keep adding stock and stirring constantly until gravy is smooth. Use the hand whisk if desired. Stir in the wine.

Simmer about 5 minutes. Taste and season if any extra salt or pepper is needed. Pour into a gravy boat or jug.

*Gluten free: Use plain gluten-free four or fine rice flour.

An old-fashioned gravy makes a roast. Or you can simply simmer some beef stock, red wine and a little red currant jelly to a smooth, slightly sweet sauce.

What went wrong

- Oily looking – be sure to drain the excess oil from the roasting pan and just use the meat juices and sticky bits for great flavour without the oiliness.
- Tasteless—undersimmered (no time for the flavours to mingle).
- Too thin and watery or gluggy and too thick.
- Burnt flavour—be careful when simmering that you remember to stir so it doesn't catch!

White Sauce

EQUIPMENT

scales and or measuring cups, liquid measuring jug, small heavy-based
saucepan, wooden spoon or silicon spatula, small balloon whisk

INGREDIENTS

30g (1oz) butter
2 tablespoons plain (all-purpose) flour (or rice flour for a gluten-free sauce)
350ml (12fl oz) milk (full cream or low fat)
salt flakes and freshly ground black pepper
good pinch ground nutmeg

*Variation: Instead of 350ml (12fl oz) milk, use 175ml (6fl oz) millk
and 175ml (6fl oz) chicken stock*

METHOD

Melt the butter in the saucepan over a medium heat until foamy (do not
burn).

Add in the flour and stir constantly for 2 minutes, or until the mixture is
a sandy colour (this is called a roux). Make sure the mixture doesn't burn.

Remove the pan from the heat. Add the milk and whisk in quickly. Put
the pan back onto the heat. Bring to the boil over a medium low heat,
stirring constantly until the sauce thickens and bubbles appear (about 4
minutes).

Don't stop stirring!

Season well with the nutmeg and salt and pepper.

*Tip: To make this into a cheese sauce, just stir through ½ cup
of grated tasty or cheddar cheese in the last minute of cooking
time and stir well. Or try a combination of tasty or cheddar and
parmesan for a bit of extra bite!*

What went wrong

- Burning or overcooking the roux—this will make the sauce brown and taste burnt.
- Adding too much flour will make it thick and possibly lumpy.
- Leaving the sauce too long before using will cause a nasty skin to form on top.
- Too much butter (sauce will be oily).
- Not enough whisking or stirring (lumps and sauce catch and burn on the base of the pan.
- Flour-butter mixture (roux) not cooked enough (sauce will taste floury).

Creamy Mayonnaise

Makes 300ml (10½fl oz)

EQUIPMENT
food processor, liquid measuring jug, lemon juicer, tablespoons

INGREDIENTS
1 large whole egg and 3 yolks (at room temperature)
sea salt
200ml (7fl oz/¾ cup) pure olive oil
125ml (4fl oz/½ cup) extra light olive oil (extra light will lighten the flavour)
juice of ½ lemon (about 3 tablespoons)
good 2–3 teaspoons Dijon mustard
2 tablespoons cream (this adds a luscious texture and lightens the texture)
freshly ground black pepper, to taste

METHOD
Add the whole egg, yolks and salt to the food processor. Process 10 seconds.

Add the oil very, very slowly (literally drop by drop) through the chute on the processor (you must be very slow initially until the mayonnaise starts to thicken).

Once the mayonnaise is starting to thicken you can add the oil in a slow steady stream. (But still be patient). Then, once thick, the oil can flow quite quickly.

Add the lemon, mustard, cream and season with the salt and pepper.

Store in a sealed container in the refrigerator and add your own bit of love to salads, potatoes, chicken, sandwiches and anything else you like! Keeps for up to one week.

Tip: If the mixture will simply not thicken you have added the oil too quickly, some say add egg yolks and it will thicken, but I don't think this works. Throw it out and start again! For a thick mayonnaise you may like to leave out the lemon juice or the cream or both.

What went wrong

- Cold eggs (eggs for cooking should always be at room temperature—warm them up by popping them into some warm water for about 5 minutes if it's a cold day!)
- Not enough quantity for the processor or blade to pick up. I always use at least 3 eggs.
- Oil! Think about the flavour of the oil. Don't use strong or flavoured oils, keep it basic— olive oil is the best (I like to use a mix of extra virgin and extra light).
- Curdled—adding the oil too quickly.
- Underseasoned (often mayonnaise simply needs salt to make it extra special).
- Sugar—NO, not in a homemade mayonnaise; often the commercial ones are very sweet.

Basil Pesto

Makes approximately 2 cups

EQUIPMENT
scales, cook's knife, chopping board, liquid measuring jug, food processor

INGREDIENTS
200g (7oz) piece parmesan cheese (preferably a good-quality one)
100g (3½oz) pine nuts (or walnuts)
1 large clove garlic, peeled
1 large bunch fresh basil, leaves picked from the stalks (super fresh and packed with flavour)
200ml (7fl oz/¾ cup) extra virgin olive oil (you can add extra if you like the pesto thinner)
sea salt and freshly ground black pepper to taste

METHOD
Cut the parmesan into long pieces. Finely grate in the food processor. Remove and set aside—this will retain more texture in the pesto.

Add the pine nuts, garlic and basil to the processor with the chopping blade. Pulse until just chopped.

Add the oil, salt and pepper, and pulse until combined. Return the parmesan to the processor and quickly pulse. Make sure you don't overprocess—you still want to see the separate ingredients like the bits of nut and slivers of parmesan.

Remember to season the pesto well with salt and pepper, and keep tasting until it's just right.

Tip: In the cooler months, it's sometimes hard to find fresh basil. Use coriander or fresh rocket instead for a nice change.

A fresh zingy add on—perfect dolloped or drizzled over pastas, salads, pizzas, fish or chicken and so simple to whizz up. You'll never beat homemade.

What went wrong

- Overprocessing and chopping too much (takes out all the texture).
- Cheap quality, pre-grated parmesan. Definitely buy the best you can afford and grate yourself.
- Shrivelled or slimy herbs. They have lost their joy. Always use gorgeous, fresh and fragrant herbs (see A bit about herbs storage in Introduction).

Cheat's Custard

Makes 500ml (17½fl oz/2 cups)

EQUIPMENT
scales, liquid measuring jug, small heavy-based saucepan, wooden spoon or silicon spatula, small balloon whisk, small bowl, serving jug or bowl, plastic wrap or film

. . . .

INGREDIENTS
500ml (17½fl oz/2 cups) milk

2 tablespoons (40g/1½oz) caster (superfine) sugar

2 teaspoons vanilla extract

1½ tablespoons (20g/²/₃oz) custard powder (you can add another teaspoon—but don't use too much or the sauce will be too thick)

2 tablespoons cream

Smooth and glossy, just thickened custard (meaning it looks like a real one) is possible using a custard powder. Just follow these tips.

METHOD

Place about three-quarters of the milk, sugar and vanilla in the pan. Bring to a gentle boil

Place the remaining milk into a small bowl with the custard powder, stir gently to a smooth sauce (this is called a slurry).

Stirring the warm milk, pour in the custard mixture. Using the small whisk (or a wooden spoon), stir constantly over a medium low heat for 3–4 minutes until the mixture thickens and starts to boil.

Stir in the cream and stir until ready to serve. Pour into a jug or bowl and place a small sheet of plastic wrap directly onto the surface to prevent a nasty skin from forming.

Tip: Custard powder can be replaced with cornflour and a couple of drops of yellow food colouring if you like.

What went wrong

- Not measuring the ingredients correctly (too much liquid—it will be runny; too much custard powder and it will be gluggy and stodgy).
- Choose a custard powder that is not fluoro yellow (the yellow colouring is only a colour, it doesn't add any flavour).
- Heat too high—stay on medium heat or the milk will burn.
- Not enough whisking and stirring—instant lumps and sauce catches and burns on the base of the pan.
- Sauce not cooked enough (make sure you have steam and some bubbles gently appearing please).

Baking

Perfect Sponge Sandwich

Serves 6

EQUIPMENT

scales or measuring cups and measuring spoons, standmixer with whisk attachment, small mixing bowls, small hand whisk, spatula, large metal spoon, 2 x 20cm (8in) cake pans, scissors, cooling rack

. . . .

INGREDIENTS

135g (4½oz/1 cup) plain (all-purpose) flour (or gluten-free plain flour)
2 tablespoons cornflour (cornstarch)
1½ teaspoons baking powder
4 at room temperature, large eggs
¾ cup caster (superfine) sugar
3 tablespoons boiling water
1 teaspoon butter
your favourite jam, to serve
sweetened thickened cream, to serve

METHOD

Measure the ingredients perfectly. Arrange the oven shelves (bake a sponge on the lower middle shelf).

Preheat the oven to 180°C (350°F) (fan off preferably or 160°C (320°F) if fan forced–see page 16).

Grease the bottom and sides of the cake pans. Lightly flour the side and line the bottom with a circle of baking paper (see page 24).

Place the flours and baking powder in a small bowl and, using a little whisk, combine well, set aside (I am a lazy cook and NOT a fan of sifting, this little cheating method works well).

Place the eggs and sugar into a mixing bowl on your standmixer. Turn to high speed (10) and whisk at least

8 minutes until very thick and creamy (the mixture will fall back on itself and hold its shape if tested; this is called forming a ribbon).

Just before the eggs and sugar are ready, stir the butter into the boiling water. Turn off the mixer and remove bowl from mixer. Shower/scatter in the flour mixture lightly and pour the boiling water down the side of the bowl (remember to work quickly).

Using a large metal spoon fold the mixture together by cutting the edge of the spoon through the creamy mixture and folding it over itself gently. Do not overmix it.

Divide the mixture evently between the pans (I weigh each pan on a set of scales).

Put the two tins quickly into the oven, side by side. Work quickly but calmly—no dawdling and mucking around please! Close the oven door carefully (many believe slamming the door lets out too much air and the sponge will sink).

Set the timer and bake 20 minutes. Remove from the oven and let stand for 3 minutes before turning out of the pans onto cooling racks. Remove the paper from the base and allow to cool (don't turn out too quickly as if the sponges are too hot, they will stick to the cake rack).

When completely cool, spread one cake with your favourite jam, top with a dollop of whipped cream and gently spread out to the sides. Top with fresh berries if desired and carefully place the other cake on top.

Dust with icing sugar to serve and it's perfect!

Feather-light and soft. The most delicious simple cake filled with your favourite jam and slightly sweetened cream. Heaven!

What went wrong

- Not weighing ingredients properly (the ratio of eggs to sugar to flour is very important).
- Buttering tins very well (yes I prefer to use butter. I keep the wrappers from the butter just for this job)
- The incorrect tins (and make sure they are perfectly washed and dried).
- Line the base only with circle of baking paper, not the sides for a sponge (the outside edge will be removed when you remove the baking paper).
- Overmixing—this will remove the precious air you have whisked in and give you a dry, sunken cake.
- Uneven amounts placed in tins (I weigh them to make sure they are even)!
- Under- or overbaking—removing the sponge cake from the oven before it is firm means you will have gooey spots.

Buttery Shortbread

Makes around 22 shortbread

EQUIPMENT

scales and/or metric cup measures and measuring spoons, food processor fitted with a chopping/all-purpose blade, spatula, plastic wrap, baking paper, rolling pin, baking tray, chopping board, cook's knife, cooling rack, spatula or egg slide

. . . .

INGREDIENTS

185g (6oz) cultured, unsalted chilled butter, roughly chopped into large cubes

75g (½ cup) icing (confectioners') sugar

1 teaspoon vanilla extract

135g (1 cup) plain (all-purpose) flour (or gluten-free plain flour)

75g (½ cup) fine rice flour or cornflour (cornstarch)

little extra plain (all-purpose) flour for dusting hands and bench

Tips: Choose unsalted butter or salt-reduced for baking. Buy the best butter you can! Better quality butters are sold in a foil wrapper. Foil-wrapped butters tend to have less water and therefore produce a much better result. Use a food processor! It gives a great finish. Making by hand can mean overworking, oiling and toughening the dough.

METHOD

Weigh or measure the ingredients correctly, incorrect measurements of butter of flour can cause bad results in biscuits!

Preheat the oven to 160°C (320°F) (140°C (285°F) fan-forced). Pop the oven shelf into the bottom third of the oven.

Line a baking sheet with baking paper.

Place the chilled butter, icing sugar and vanilla into the food processor. Pulse for 6–8 seconds to cream together.

Add both flours and pulse 10 seconds or until mixture is combined. Do not expect mixture to form a ball: it will not.

Lightly dust the bench top with the extra flour. Remove the mixture with a spatula and form into a blob on the bench. Lightly knead until just smooth (be careful not to overwork the mixture).

Form into a log shape and roll in plastic wrap. Refrigerate for 30 minutes (this rests the mixture and helps to produce a soft, tender result).

Slice into discs approx. 5mm thick. Each disc can then be cut into a pretty shape if desired. Arrange on the lined baking tray, leaving a small gap in between each. (The 'cut-offs' can be rerolled into a log, rested as above and made into more shortbread.)

Bake for 20 minutes or until just firm when pressed lightly with your finger. Remove tray from oven and allow shortbreads to rest 5 minutes to firm before carefully removing to a cooling rack to cool completely.

The dough can be made ahead and refrigerated for up to one week. Freeze the log for up to three months. Soften the frozen dough for 15 minutes or until it can be cut without breaking. If the mixture is very cold the biscuits will take an extra few minutes to bake.

What went wrong

- Incorrect measurements—this is very important with biscuits. If this delicate balance is not correct the biscuits can spread into flat pancakes.
- Incorrect oven temperature.
- 'Oiling' and melting the butter into the flour (this produces a dense, cakey biscuit).
- Overmixing the dough (this toughens the dough).
- Not refrigerating and resting the dough (the dough will be tough, as the flour proteins need to relax).

Fluffy Muffins

Makes 6 large or 8 small

EQUIPMENT

scales or measuring cups and measuring spoons, large mixing bowl, smaller mixing bowl, hand whisk, spatula or large metal spoon, muffin pan

INGREDIENTS

1½ cups (215g/7oz) plain (all-purpose) flour (or gluten-free plain flour or see gluten-free section in Introduction)
3 teaspoons baking powder
good pinch cinnamon
½ cup caster (110g/3¹/₃oz) sugar
2 large eggs
1 x 200g (7oz) tub natural yoghurt (or you can also use milk and 1 teaspoon white vinegar)
125g (4oz) butter, melted and cooled

FLAVOURS

¼ cup chocolate chips
2 tablespoons cocoa (added to the flour mixture) plus 2 tablespoons chopped pecans
2 ripe pears or peaches, peeled and diced

It can seem such a simple thing but so often done badly. Once you get muffins right you'll be critiquing the ones at your local café in no time.

METHOD

Preheat the oven to hot: 190°C (375°F) (170°C/340°F fan forced).

Butter the sides of the muffin pan.

Always use paper liners! Pop a liner into each hole of the muffin pan.

Combine all the dry ingredients in a mixing bowl and with a whisk stir to combine well.

Place the wet ingredients (eggs, yoghurt or milk and butter) in the smaller mixing bowl and whisk.

When the oven is hot, liners ready … pour the wet whisked ingredients into the dry ingredients. Using a large metal spoon fold them together until JUST mixed. It's good if the batter is still a little uneven and lumpy). DO NOT OVERMIX.

Spoon the batter into the muffin holes—only fill around ¾ to the top.

Quickly place in the oven and bake 20 minutes or until firm.

FLAVOURS

Add the dry flavours like cocoa and nuts to the flour and the wet ingredients like diced fruit to the egg mixture.

Tip: This recipe can be made in your standmixer, just make sure you don't overmix. Lumps are essential for a gorgeous muffin.

What went wrong

- Not measuring ingredients correctly.
- Too much liquid makes a pointed, peaked muffin.
- Too much sugar (little crusted spots appear on the surface).
- Adding hot butter, will make the muffin oily and dense.
- Overmixing (this makes mixture tough and incorporating too much air will also make the muffins peak).
- Overfilling (muffin will mushroom over the pan).

Pavlova

Serves 6-8

EQUIPMENT

scales or measuring cups, standmixer with whisk attachment, spatula, kitchen timer, oven tray, baking paper, egg slide or flat spatula

. . . .

INGREDIENTS

4 large egg whites, at room temperature
pinch salt
1¼ cups (225g/8oz) caster (superfine) sugar
1 teaspoon white vinegar
1 teaspoon cornflour (cornstarch)
2 teaspoons vanilla extract (optional)
1 tablespoon boiling water

Recipe can be doubled for a larger meringue.

METHOD

Line an oven tray with baking paper, draw a 20cm (7¾in) circle on the paper to act as a guide for the meringue. Preheat the oven to 190°C (375°F), adjust oven shelf to the lower one-third of the oven. Preferably with no fan; however if you only have a fan-forced oven reduce the temperature to 170°C (340°F).

Use large eggs and ALWAYS at room temperature. No egg yolk to be present (not a skerrick!).

Weigh and measure ingredients correctly. Make sure the mixing bowl and whisk on your standmixer is clean and very dry.

Whisk the egg whites and salt on low speed (speed 2) until soft peaks form. Increase the speed to high (10) and add about one-third of the sugar, showering it into the bowl. Continue whisking/beating until the sugar has dissolved, about 3 minutes. Add another one-third of the sugar and continue beating. Repeat, adding the remaining last batch of sugar. Make sure the sugar is completely dissolved. You might need to quickly turn off the mixer and wipe down the sides of the bowl. Rub a small amount of meringue in between your fingers to check it is smooth and without any grainy feeling.

With the mixer turned off, add the vinegar, cornflour and vanilla. Pour the boiling water down the side of the bowl. Turn on the mixer to the lowest speed and gently combine the ingredients. Do not overmix.

Pile the meringue onto the prepared tray and gently smooth the sides and top, without 'playing' with the mixture too much (as it will lose volume).

Place into the oven and bake 5 minutes at this high temperature, then reduce temperature to 100°C (210°F) and bake for 1½ hours.

Turn off the oven but leave the meringue in the oven to completely cool (some say to leave the door ajar, I think allowing any air into the oven assists the shell in further cracking and the middle to sink badly).

Transfer the meringue to a serving dish or airtight container if storing. Top with sweetened whipped cream and your favourite fruit to serve.

Tip: Meringue shell should keep well for up to three days in an airtight container in a cool dark place.

What went wrong

- Incorrect measuring (the sugar to egg ratio is important).
- Any egg yolk present in the whites (limits volume).
- Wet or oily bowl or whisk (limits volume).
- Cold egg straight from the fridge (aeration is limited).
- Using the wrong sugar (use caster (superfine) sugar not A1 standard sugar).
- UNDERBEATING! If the sugar is not beaten in until completely dissolved it will cause the pavlova to weep pools of sugar syrup.
- Interrupting the mixing, or taking too long to pile meringue onto tray, work quickly! The mixture thins out as air is lost.
- Overmixing once cornflour and or vinegar is added (mixture thins out).
- Opening the oven door or cooling too quickly (meringue sinks).
- Rainy days (yes it causes chaos as high humidity affects meringues creating increased danger of weeping and severe cracking).

Family Chocolate Cake

Serves 8–12

EQUIPMENT

scales or measuring cups and measuring spoons, 20cm (8in) high-sided cake pan, small hand whisk, mixing bowl, scissors, standmixer with flat beater attachment, spatula, cooling rack

. . . .

INGREDIENTS

2 cups (270g/9½oz) self-raising (self-rising) flour (or gluten-free plain flour, see Gluten-free section in Introduction)

½ cup (80g/2½oz) dark cocoa

185g (6oz) unsalted or salt-reduced butter, at room temperature

1 cup (250g/9oz) caster (superfine) sugar

1 teaspoon vanilla extract

½ cup (80g/2½oz) brown sugar

3 large eggs, room temperature

250ml (9fl oz) room temperature milk combined with 2 teaspoons white vinegar

2 tablespoons natural yoghurt or sour cream

2 tablespoons boiling water

A great cake for every family occasion. It'll be the good ole standby in no time.

METHOD

Preheat the oven to 180°C (350°F) (160°C/320°F fan-forced), place the oven shelf just below the centre of the oven.

Butter/grease a high-sided 20cm (8in) round cake pan. Line the base with a circle of baking paper and the sides with thick strips of baking paper. Be sure to allow the baking paper to come 2cm (¾in) above the sides of the cake pan.

Place the flour and cocoa into a small bowl and stir until well combined with a small hand whisk (if preferred you can sift the ingredients through a fine sieve—but I find this takes too long).

Beat the butter, caster (superfine) sugar and vanilla on high speed in a standmixer for 2 minutes, add the brown sugar and beat a further 3 minutes or until very light and fluffy. Using a spatula wipe the sides of the bowl down once or twice during the creaming.

Add the eggs one at a time, beating well after each egg.

Turn off the mixer. Add the flour cocoa mixture, milk and sour cream or yoghurt. Turn to speed 1 and mix 5 seconds or until just combined. Add the boiling water, increase to speed 2 and mix a further 5 seconds or until combined. Do not overmix.

Pour the batter into the prepared pan and smooth the top with the spatula.

Bake on the centre shelf for about 1 hour 15 minutes. Cake is cooked when it's firm to touch.

Remove cake from oven and wait 5 minutes before turning out onto a cooling rack. Peel off baking paper and allow to cool completely before serving.

Dust with cocoa or icing sugar to serve. Can also be topped with a chocolate frosting to serve. See Real Chocolate Icing recipe.

What went wrong

- Not measuring ingredients properly.
- Using cold butter to cream the butter and sugar (the mixture will not increase in volume or become light and fluffy).
- Not creaming the butter and sugar enough. This gives a poor volume to the cake.
- Adding cold eggs will cause the mixture to curdle and will reduce the volume.
- Adding the eggs without thoroughly beating in after each addition (poor volume)
- Overmixing once the flour is added means the cake looses air and becomes tough.
- Incorrect oven temperature means the cake overcooks or undercooks and cracks badly.
- Incorrectly-sized cake pan—pan too big, the cake will overcook and be too shallow, become dry. Pan too small, mixture will overflow or you will have an issue cooking to the centre of the cake.

Simple Shortcrust Pastry with Lemon Filling

Makes 1 medium-sized tart shell

EQUIPMENT

scales or measuring cups and measuring spoons, food processor with multi-purpose (chopping) blade, plastic wrap, 22cm (8½in) flan tin, rolling pin, baking paper, baking weights or rice for blind baking, baking sheet

INGREDIENTS

1¾ cups (255g/8oz) plain (all-purpose) flour
2 tablespoons pure icing (confectioners') sugar
pinch salt
185g (6oz) unsalted butter, chilled
1 egg yolk
1 tablespoon ice cold water
little extra flour for your hands

SIMPLE LEMON FILLING

2 teaspoons finely grated lemon rind
3 large lemons, for 100ml (3½fl oz) lemon juice
⅓ cup (80g/2½oz) caster (superfine) sugar
4 large eggs, at room temperature
1 teaspoon vanilla extract
100ml (3½fl oz) cream (thickened or pouring)

METHOD

Weigh and measure the ingredients correctly. Chop the butter and return it to the refrigerator, to chill well (until you are ready to use it).

Place the flour, sugar and salt into the processor and pulse until combined (don't bother sifting, the processor will combine the dry ingredients perfectly). With the motor running, quickly drop the chilled butter down the chute into the flour. Once the flour is added, add the egg yolk and water and process in short bursts or pulse until it looks like it's coming together (do not over process, as it quickly becomes tough).

Take off the cover and test a small amount of dough between your fingertips, if it easily forms a soft dough, it's ready.

Very lightly flour your hands and remove the pastry, forming it into a ball. Lay a sheet of plastic wrap on the bench, place in the soft dough. Roll up and refrigerate for a minimum for 20 minutes.

Meanwhile, preheat the oven to 200°C (400°F)(180°C (350°F) fan forced) and add the baking sheet to the oven to preheat— popping the tart shell onto the hot tray will help to cook the bottom—no one likes a soggy bottom!

Remove the dough from the fridge, if it feels too firm, set aside for 5 minutes (the dough should feel like firm putty). Place the dough between two sheets of baking paper. Press the dough out to a a round flat large circle. Using the rolling pin roll out the dough going from the centre of the circle to the outside edge (try NOT to roll over the edge as this can cause shrinking). Turn the paper around to the left with each roll, so you end up moving around the circle rolling, it out from the centre. Forming a good round shape. Place a 22cm (8½in) tart tin in the centre of pastry (the pastry should be slightly larger than the flan).

Place another sheet of baking paper over the pastry-lined flan (allowing it to come up over the pasty) and fill with baking weights.

Place the filled shell into the oven (on the centre shelf on top of the baking tray) and bake 20 minutes, carefully remove the paper and beans and return the shell to the oven for about another 8–10 minutes or until it is very lightly golden brown. Allow to cool. You can fill with whipped cream and fresh strawberries or the simple lemon filling.

SIMPLE LEMON FILLING

Combine all ingredients in a standmixer with the whisk attachment (or in a bowl with a small balloon whisk). Whisk until well combined and lightly foamy. Reduce oven to 140°C (285°F). Carefully fill shell with filling and bake for around 20 minutes until just firm with a little wobble. Remove from oven, dust with icing sugar and serve.

159

What went wrong

- Butter too soft or lightly melted (this will cause the pastry to be doughy and dense).
- Too much butter: the butter does add flavour and wonderful shortness, but too much makes the pastry hard to work with (and melts easily).
- Plain (all-purpose) flour only for a crisp pastry (self-raising will give a spongy texture).
- Working with hot hands, taking tooooooooooo long and playing around with the pastry. The golden rule is keep all chilled—including your hands and work quickly.
- Over-working the pastry (this makes it tough).
- Not resting in the refrigerator before rolling (the pastry will shrink on baking)
- Pushing and pulling the pastry when rolling—try to roll in the one direction and don't go over the edges.
- Not blind-baking (eek a soggy bottomed tart).
- Oven temperature too hot (the pastry will dry and scorch and be hard and too crisp).

Choc Chip Cookies

EQUIPMENT

*scales and or metric cup measures and measuring spoons,
spatula, standmixer with beater attachment, plastic wrap, baking paper,
rolling pin, baking tray, chopping board, cook's knife, cooling rack*

INGREDIENTS

¾ cup (112g) brown sugar

¾ cup (165g) caster (superfine) sugar

*250g (9oz) unsalted butter, very well softened—it should squish very easily
between your fingertips*

1 teaspoon vanilla extract

1 large egg, at room temperature

*3 cups (405g) plain (all-purpose) flour (or gluten-free flour see recipe in
Gluten-free section in Introduction)*

2 tablespoons dark cocoa

pinch ground cinnamon

1 cup (150g/5oz) chop-chips

METHOD

Weigh or measure the ingredients correctly, incorrect measurements of
butter of flour can cause bad results in biscuits!

Preheat the oven to 160°C (320°F) (140°C/285°F fan-forced), arrange
the oven shelves to the bottom third of the oven.

Line two baking sheets with baking paper.

Place the sugars, butter, vanilla, egg, flour, cocoa, cinnamon and choc
chips into your standmixer. Using the beater attachment, mix on low
speed (1) until the mixture comes together. Increase the speed to medium
(4) and beat for 1 minute.

Take tablespoon amounts and roll into a balls. Place on the lined trays,
allowing for spreading.

Bake 20 minutes or until firm. Remove tray from oven and allow
shortbreads to rest 5 minutes to firm before carefully removing to a
cooling rack to cool completely.

Makes approximately 25 biscuits

What went wrong

- Incorrect measurements—this is very important with biscuits! If this delicate balance is not correct the biscuits can spread into flat pancakes.
- Incorrect oven temperature (too hot the biscuit will dry on the outside and not cook evenly).
- 'Oily-ing' and melting the butter into the flour (this produces a dense, cakey biscuit).
- Overmixing the dough (this toughens the dough).

Tip: Use your standmixer, it produces a wonderful result. Making by hand can result in overworking, oiling and toughening.

Cocoa Brownies

Makes 12

EQUIPMENT

scales, liquid cup and spoon measurements, small heavy-based saucepan, spatula, standmixer with mixing bowl, beater attachment, 20cm (8in) square cake pan

. . . .

INGREDIENTS

250g (9oz) unsalted butter, chopped and very soft

75g (2½oz/¾ cups) dark cocoa (I prefer Dutch cocoa)

135g (4½oz/1 cup) plain (all-purpose) flour (or gluten-free plain flour see recipe in Gluten-free section in Introduction)

165g (¾ cup/5½oz) raw sugar

60g (¼ cup) caster (superfine) sugar

4 large eggs (at room temperature please)

1 teaspoon vanilla extract

2 teaspoons finely grated orange zest

110g (3½oz/1 cup) walnuts (or substitute with 1 cup of pecans)

extra cocoa for dusting

A little square of gooey chocolately deliciousness ... it's hard to stop at just one!

METHOD

Preheat the oven to 180°C (350°F). Butter and line the base and sides of a 20cm square cake pan.

Combine the cocoa and flour in a small bowl and using a little whisk, combine well, set aside (I am a lazy cook and NOT a fan of sifting, this little cheating method works well).

Place the sugars, eggs, vanilla and orange zest into the mixing bowl of your standmixer. Using the beater attachment, beat 1 minute on medium speed (6).

Add the butter, cocoa and flour. Beat on medium low (4) for 1 minute or until well combined. Add the nuts and mix a further 10 seconds.

Pour the mixture into your pan. Bake for 10 minutes. Remove from oven and cover with a piece of foil. Scrunch the foil tightly around the edges. Bake on the centre shelf of the oven for 15 minutes. Remove the foil and bake for a further 5 minutes. The mixture should still be a little gooey in the centre—gently stick in the end of a skewer or tip of a knife to test.

Remove from the oven (leaving the brownie in the pan), and let completely cool.

Dust heavily with the extra cocoa and cut into squares to serve.

Serve with loads of fresh berries and lashings of cream.

What went wrong

- Overcooking (brownies will be dry ... it must have squidgy-ness!
- Overmixing—don't be tempted ... tough and stiff!
- Not covering (the oven will take out the moisture—again dry dry dry and dull dull dull).

Butter Cupcakes

Makes 12

GF

EQUIPMENT

scales and/or measuring cups, measuring spoons, small bowl, small balloon whisk, citrus juicer, fine grater, standmixer with beater attachment, muffin tin with patty pans, large ice cream scoop, flat-bladed knife or piping bag

INGREDIENTS

100g (3½oz) unsalted butter, at very soft room temperature

½ cup (110g/3½oz) caster (superfine) sugar

2 large eggs, at room temperature

1 teaspoon vanilla extract (optional) (I love vanilla so always add this, if I have a vanilla bean pod, I spilt it, scrape out the seeds and add them)

1 cup (135g) self-raising (self-rising) flour (or gluten-free flour, see recipe in Gluten-free section in Introduction)

2 tablespoons (45g) sour cream or vanilla yoghurt

ICING

½ cup (60g/2oz) icing (confectioners') sugar (this makes a smooth creamy icing—for a firmer icing, quantity can be doubled)

70g (2¼oz) unsalted butter, at very soft room temperature

1 teaspoon lemon or orange juice (pulp free)

½ teaspoon finely grated lemon or orange rind (this adds a little extra flavour boost)

METHOD

Preheat the oven to 180°C (350°F). Place medium-sized patty cases into a 12-hole cupcake pan. Place the oven shelf in the bottom third of the oven.

Place the butter, sugar and vanilla into the mixing bowl on your standmixer. Turn to medium high speed (8) and beat with the beater attachment for at least 5 minutes or until light and creamy. This beating is giving the cake a soft texture and good volume.

Add the eggs one at a time beating well in between each addition. Make sure the mixture is creamy and fluffy before adding the next egg.

Add the flour and sour cream and mix on low (speed 1) for about 15 seconds or until combined.

Fill each patty cake with about 2 tablespoons batter (I like to use an old fashioned ice-cream scoop).

Bake 18 minutes until firm (touch lightly with your fingertip) and golden brown.

Stand 5 minutes before removing from pan. Place on a cooling rack and cool completely before icing.

ICING

Place the ingredients in the bowl of your standmixer. Beat on medium high (speed 6) for 5 minutes or until light and fluffy. Spread the icing on with a flat bladed knife or use a piping bag.

What went wrong

- Not weighing ingredients properly. The ratio of dry ingredients to butter and eggs is important—incorrect measuring affects the texture and consistency of the batter and the shape of the cakes when cooked.
- Butter must be at room temperature (if it's cold it will not beat into the mixture—this step adds the volume to the cakes).
- Too much sugar (cakes will be crusty on top with sugar speckles and can have dark spots).
- Too much liquid (the cakes will peak—not be rounded and smooth).
- Too much beating (the cakes can puff up then sink, and the cake will toughen if over-beaten)
- Too much batter added to the pan or patty cases (the cakes will mushroom and spill).

Melting Moments

Makes approximately 20 sandwiched biscuits

EQUIPMENT

scales and/or metric cup measures and measuring spoons, standmixer with beater attachment, spatula, plastic wrap, baking paper, rolling pin, baking tray, chopping board, cook's knife, cooling rack, spatula or lifter

. . . .

INGREDIENTS

160g (1 cup/4½oz) pure icing (confectioners') sugar
215g (7oz/1½ cups) plain (all-purpose) flour (or gluten-free plain flour or see gluten-free section in Introduction)
80g (2½oz/½ cup) cornflour
250g (9oz) cultured unsalted butter (roughly chopped, at a soft room temperature)
1 teaspoon vanilla extract
little extra plain (all-purpose) flour for dusting hands

LEMON BUTTER CREAM

75g (2½oz) unsalted butter, at a soft room temperature
80g (2½oz/½ cup) icing (confectioners') sugar
3 teaspoons finely grated lemon rind

A little buttery joy filled with a tangy lemon icing that dances on your tongue.

METHOD

Weigh or measure the ingredients correctly, incorrect measurements of butter or flour can cause bad results in biscuits.

Preheat the oven to 160°C (320°F) (140°C/285°F fan-forced), arrange the oven shelfs to the lower half of the oven. Line two oven trays with sheets of baking paper.

Place the icing sugar in a small bowl and using a little whisk combine well then divide in half reserving half for the butter cream—this little cheating method works well.

Combine flour and cornflour in another small bowl. Using the balloon whisk, combine these. Set aside.

Put the butter and vanilla into your standmixer bowl. Using the beater attachment, beat on low speed (speed 2) for 30 seconds.

Add the icing sugar. Turn to medium high (speed 8) and beat 5 minutes until very light and fluffy. (During the mixing, stop the mixer and wipe down the sides of the bowl with a spatula.)

Add the combined flours, turn to low (speed 1) and mix 30 seconds or until just combined.

Lightly flour your fingertips (and be gentle the mixture is soft). Take about 1 tablespoon amount, roll into a ball and place on the prepared tray. Leave some room between for spreading. Press gently on each one with the back of a fork, dipped regularly in flour to prevent sticking, to flatten slightly.

Bake 12–15 minutes (until just firm and golden). Stand 5 minutes before carefully moving each biscuit to a cooling rack to cool completely. When cool, sandwich together with butter cream,

LEMON BUTTER CREAM

Combine the ingredients in your clean, dry standmixer bowl. Using the beater beat 5 minutes (until lovely and light and fluffy)

Tip: Buy the best butter you can. Cultured butter has a culture added to it. This softens the crumb and gives a delicious flavour to the biscuits. Or choose unsalted butter or salt reduced. (Better quality butters are sold in a foil wrapper. Foil-wrapped butters tend to have less water and therefore produce a much better result.)

What went wrong

- Overmixing (bickies will be tough and have a stodgy texture).
- Undercooking (bickies will have a slightly floury taste and will look too light).
- Overcooking (dry texture to the bickies with overbrowned bits).
- Lumpy icing (need I say more? Yuk!).
- Not enough icing (the ratio between biscuit and icing is important ... make them with love!).

Coconut Bars (Lamingtons)

Makes 15

EQUIPMENT

scales and or measuring cups, measuring spoons, small bowl, small balloon whisk, measuring jug, 22cm (8½in) cake pan, cooling rack, heatproof bowl, medium-sized saucepan, serrated knife, shallow bowl, 2 forks, large sheet baking paper

· ·

INGREDIENTS

1½ cups (225g/8oz) self-raising (self-rising) flour (or gluten-free flour or see gluten-free section in Introduction)

⅓ cup (40g/1½oz) cornflour

180g (6oz) unsalted butter, at room temperature

¾ cup (150g/5oz) caster (superfine) sugar

3 large eggs, at room temperature

1 teaspoon vanilla

½ cup (125ml/4oz) milk, room temperature, mixed with 1 teaspoon vinegar

ICING AND DECORATING

4 cups (500g/17½oz) icing (confectioners') sugar mixture

⅔ cup (80g/2½oz) cocoa powder

1 tablespoon (20g/⅔oz) butter, room temperature

200ml (7fl oz) milk, room temperature

3 cups (285g/10oz) desiccated coconut

METHOD

Preheat the oven to 180°C (350°F). Grease and baking paper line the base and sides of a 22cm (8in) deep square cake pan. Arrange the oven shelf in the bottom third of the oven.

Place the flour and cornflour into the mixing bowl on your standmixer. Using the beater attachment, mix 10 seconds on low (speed 1). Add the butter, sugar, eggs, vanilla and milk. Beat on low speed 1 for 10 seconds, increase speed to medium (speed 6) then to medium high (speed 8) and beat for 2 minutes or until batter is thick and creamy.

Pour the batter into the pan and smooth over the top (don't leave any peakie bits).

Bake 50 minutes or until firm and golden (very lightly touch the surface with your fingertip, it will feel just firm).

Stand 10 minutes before removing from pan. Carefully place the cake on a cooling rack and cool completely.

While the cake is cooling, make the icing: place the icing sugar mixture and cocoa in a medium-sized heatproof bowl and mix with a small balloon whisk until lump-free and combined. Add the butter and milk. Place the bowl over a saucepan of simmering hot water. Stir slowly for about 3 minutes until the icing is smooth and glossy. Remove the bowl from the heat and set aside.

Spread the coconut into the centre of a sheet of baking paper.

Using a serrated knife, trim off the very outside edge and cut the cake into 16 squares. (I like them very square and all the same size.)

Using two forks, carefully but quickly dunk a square of cake into the icing, lightly coating it all over. Place it onto the coconut and gently roll and sprinkle to coat evenly. Place on a cake rack. Repeat with the remaining cake squares.

What went wrong

- Incorrect measuring (particularly too little sugar, or too much milk) will ruin the texture of the cake.
- Incorrect oven temperature (too low cake will be pale and dense, too high cake will cook unevenly be hard on the outside edge and not cooked in the centre).
- Overmixing (this toughens the batter).
- Not spreading batter evenly into the pan (you'll end up with an uneven cake).
- Too high a shelf placement (the cake will dry and crack).
- Lumpy, too dry or too runny icing will ruin the look of the lamington and you will end up applying too much or too little.
- Inconsistent sizing.

Little Lemon Cakes

Makes 6

EQUIPMENT

scales, 6 mini loaf cake pans, standmixer, measuring cups,
liquid measuring jug, spatula

. . . .

INGREDIENTS

250g (9oz) unsalted cultured butter, at very soft room
temperature (buy the best you can afford)

1 cup (220g/7½oz) caster (superfine) sugar

2 teaspoons vanilla extract

4 large eggs, at room temperature

2 cups (270g/10oz) self-raising (self-rising) flour (or gluten-
free flour—see the gluten-free section in the Introduction)

½ cup (80g/2½oz) almond meal

pinch salt

finely grated rind and juice 1 lemon

½ cup (125ml/4fl oz) milk, room temperature

extra icing (confectioners') sugar

*A cute, delightfully soft and moist cake
with a delicious lemon kick.*

METHOD

Preheat the oven to 180°C (350°F). Line 6 mini loaf pans, 12 x 5cm (4¾ x 2in) size with a piece of baking paper allowing it to overhand the sides (this acts like handles and makes lifting out easy).

Place the butter, sugar, vanilla and egg into the mixing bowl of your standmixer with the beater attachment. Beat on medium high speed (speed 6–8) for 7 minutes or until the mixture is very light and creamy. Wipe down the sides of the bowl a couple of times during the beating.

Turn the mixer off. Add the flour, salt, lemon rind, juice and milk. Mix on low speed (speed 1) until mixture is just combined about 10 seconds—the mixture may slightly curdle due to the lemon juice, don't worry about this.

Divide the mixture into the pans, smooth over the tops. (don't leave any peakie bits).

Place the little pans onto a baking tray. Bake 20 minutes or until firm and golden.

Stand 5 minutes before lifting the cakes from the pans. Cool on a cooling rack. Dust heavily with icing sugar.

Carefully place cakes on a cooling rack with a large tray underneath (to collect the drips). Carefully remove the paper. If icing, cool completely and then drizzle with Drippy Yoghurt Icing (see recipe, page 197). Allow the icing to set before serving.

Mini loaf baking pans are sold in cookware shops and specialty stores. A large loaf pan is approximately 22 x 12cm (8½ x 4¾in).

What went wrong

- Not weighing the ingredients properly—the ratio of dry ingredients to butter and eggs is important!
- Butter must be at room temperature—if it's cold it will not beat into the egg mixture. This step creates volume in the cakes.
- Too much sugar! The cake will be crusty on top with sugar speckles and can have dark spots.
- Too much beating once the flour is added (the cakes can puff up then sink and will be tough).
- Incorrectly sized cake pans (too large cake will be flat and overcooked, too small and the batter will overflow).
- Icing—lumps! (the icing sugar must be sifted before mixing)

Chocolate Self-saucing Pudding

Serves 6–8

EQUIPMENT

*scales, measuring cups and spoons, small saucepan or
microwave bowl, standmixer with beater attachment,
spatula, 1.2 litre (44fl oz) ovenproof dish*

. . . .

INGREDIENTS

125g (4oz) butter

*1½ cups (215g/7oz) self-raising (self-rising) flour (or gluten-
free flour, see gluten-free section in the Introduction)*

*3 tablespoons (40g/1½oz) dark baking cocoa (my favourite is
Dutch cocoa)*

⅓ cup (75g/2½oz) caster (superfine) sugar

1 tablespoon brown sugar

250ml (9fl oz/1 liquid cup) milk (preferably full cream)

1 teaspoon vanilla extract

100g (3½oz) dark cooking chocolate, roughly chopped

icing (confectioners') sugar and extra cocoa to dust

CHOCOLATE SAUCE

375ml (13oz/1½ cups) boiling water

2 tablespoons (30g/1oz) cocoa (preferably Dutch)

⅓ cup (75g/2½oz) caster (superfine) sugar

1 tablespoon brown sugar

¼ teaspoon ground cinnamon

Recipe can be halved or doubled if desired.

METHOD

Preheat the oven to 180°C (350°F) and butter a 1.25 litre (44fl oz) ovenproof dish.

Place the butter into a small saucepan (or into a microwave-safe bowl), and melt over a low heat (or 30% power in microwave).

Place the flour, cocoa and sugars into the mixing bowl of a standmixer with the beater attachment. Turn to low (speed 1) and mix until well combined (about 10 seconds).

Add the milk, butter and vanilla and mix on medium low (speed 4) for 30 seconds, add the chocolate and mix until combined.

Pour the mixture into the ovenproof dish.

CHOCOLATE SAUCE

Place a clean and dry mixing bowl on the standmixer with the beater attachment. Pour in the boiling water, add the cocoa, sugars and cinnamon.

Mix on low speed (1) for 5 seconds or until combined.

Pour the hot liquid evenly over the batter.

Bake in the oven for 40 minutes or until just firm. Dust with icing sugar and serve immediately

A simple and delicious old-fashioned wonder, with a lovely chocolatey crust on top and a gorgeous sludge of chocolate sauce underneath.

What went wrong

- Not weighing ingredients properly (the ratio of dry ingredients to butter and eggs is important).
- Butter must be cooled after melting! Adding too hot butter will produce a dense cake layer.
- Cold milk! This can set the butter in the batter, which causes little lumps.
- A dish that's too large—pudding will be too shallow and flat looking.
- Cold water! Hot water must be used for the sauce, so the cocoa dissolves, or the sauce will be lumpy.
- Measure correctly (not enough sauce will result in a dry pudding).
- Sauce is poured over the pudding! The magic of a self saucing is the sauce poured over the top becomes the sauce in the bottom.

Coconut Jam Slice

Makes 1 slab

(GF)

EQUIPMENT

16 x 26cm (6¹/₃ x 10¹/₃in) slice pan, small saucepan, mixing bowl, balloon whisk, food processor

INGREDIENTS

150g (5oz) unsalted butter

2 cups (270g/10½oz) plain (all-purpose) flour (or gluten-free flour or see Gluten-free section in Introduction)

½ teaspoon baking powder

¹/₃ cup (75g/2½oz) caster (superfine) sugar

1 large egg, at room temperature

1 cup mixed berry conserve

TOPPING

2 cups (140g/5oz) shredded coconut

2 tablespoons (30g/1oz) caster (superfine) sugar

2 tablespoons (24g/¾oz) brown sugar

2 large eggs, at room temperature

METHOD

Preheat the oven to 180°C (350°F). Line the pan with a large sheet of baking paper, allowing the sides to come up over the edges (this allows you to easily lift the slice from the pan).

Pop the butter into a small saucepan and melt gently over a medium low heat. Set aside to cool.

Combine all the flour and baking powder and salt in a bowl and using a little balloon whisk, combine together. Set aside. (I am a lazy cook and NOT a fan of sifting, this little cheating method works well.)

Place the flour, sugar, vanilla and egg into the large bowl of your food processor. Pulse, while pouring in the butter in a steady stream and continue until mixture is just sticking together and holding.

Press the dough firmly (using your fingertips) into the lined pan. Press the dough firmly into the edges of the pan.

Bake in the centre shelf of the oven for 15 minutes. Remove from the oven. Cool 5 minutes. Using the back of a spoon, spread the jam gently over the slice. Set aside.

TOPPING

Place all the ingredients into a clean dry processor bowl, cover and pulse until just combined, about 5 seconds. Don't overmix or you will chop up the coconut.

Reduce the oven temperature to 160°C (320°F). Dollop the coconut topping over the jam (leave little bits of jam showing through). Put slice carefully back into the oven and bake 20–25 minutes or until lightly golden and firm.

Stand 15 minutes before removing from pan, using the paper as handles lift out the slice. Place onto a cooling rack and cool. Cut into squares to serve.

What went wrong

- Not weighing ingredients properly—the ratio of dry ingredients to butter and eggs is important.
- Butter must be melted and cooled, not hot. Adding hot butter will make the base dense and oily.
- Eggs cold? When processed with hot butter, the eggs will curdle in the mixture.
- Incorrectly sized tin? Too small, the slice is too thick and dense, too big the slice will be overcooked and too crisp or burnt.
- Overmixing the topping (the delicious coconut will be chopped into the eggs and can curdle) and you will loose the gorgeous chunky crumble texture.

Jam Drops

Makes 10-12

EQUIPMENT

scales, measuring cups, liquid measuring jug, balloon whisk, mixing bowl, standmixer, two bicuit baking trays, wooden spoon, teaspoon, tablespoon

· ·

INGREDIENTS

1 cup (135g) self-raising (self-rising) flour
¼ cup wholemeal plain flour
pinch mixed spice
90g (3oz) unsalted butter, softened to room temperature
⅓ cup (75g/2½oz) caster (superfine) sugar
1 large egg
2 teaspoons milk
1 teaspoon vanilla extract
2 tablespoons seedy good-quality raspberry jam

I'm a real biscuit girl! These are gorgeous and golden with a little splodge of sweetness in the centre—heavenly!

What went wrong

- Too thick and dry cracked overcooked doughy biscuits.
- Not weighing ingredients properly. The ratio of dry ingredients to butter, eggs and milk is important, the biscuits can 'flood' into each other or become 'cakey' or doughy.
- Cold eggs? They will curdle within the butter, this changes the light texture of the biscuit.
- Cream the butter and sugar well; undissolved sugar will give a coarse dense texture.
- Hole/dent for jam not deep enough? The jam spills out and burns.
- Biscuits placed too close together on the tray will join together.

METHOD

Preheat the oven to 180°C (350°F). Line two biscuit trays with baking paper.

Combine the flours and spice in a small bowl and using a little balloon whisk, combine together. Set aside.

Place the butter, vanilla and sugar into a mixing bowl on your standmixer. Turn to medium high speed (8) and beat with the beater for at least 5 minutes until very thick and creamy. Rub a little mixture between your finger and thumb, the mixture should feel quite smooth.

Add the egg slowly, to the mixture and beat another 10 seconds.

Turn off the mixer. Add the flour, spices and the milk to the mixer. Beat on slow or low speed (1) mixing until flour is just combined, about 10 seconds—don't overmix.

Using two dessertspoons, drop 6 tablespoon amounts onto the tray. Space them out evenly and allow for some spreading.

Using the end of a wooden spoon, form a small hole in the top of each biscuit. Using a teaspoon pop a little bit of jam into each hole. Don't overfill as the jam with ooze out.

Place the trays into the oven (it's okay to put them on separate shelves) and bake for 12–14 minutes or until biscuits are golden.

Remove trays from the oven and let cool 5 minutes before moving. Use a flat spatula, to carefully move each biscuit to a cooling rack. Cool completely.

Marble Cake

Makes 1 large cake

EQUIPMENT

scales and/or measuring cups, measuring spoons, small bowl, small balloon whisk, measuring jug, standmixer, fluted kugelhoph or deep ring pan, cooling rack, small saucepan, wooden spoon, dinner plate

. . . .

INGREDIENTS

2 cups (270g/9½oz) plain (all-purpose) flour (or gluten-free flour, see gluten-free section in the Introduction)

⅓ cup (40g/⅔oz) cornflour

3 teaspoons baking powder

pinch salt

1 cup (220g/8oz) caster (superfine) sugar

4 large eggs, at room temperature

2 teaspoons vanilla extract (optional, I love vanilla so always add this, if I have a vanilla bean pod, I split it, scrape out the seeds and add them instead)

¾ cup (200ml/7fl oz) milk, at room temperature

2 tablespoons natural yoghurt

250g (9oz) unsalted butter, at very soft room temperature, roughly chopped

⅓ cup (50g/1¾oz) cocoa

CARAMEL ICING

1 cup light brown sugar

50g (1¾oz) butter

2 tablespoons cream

1 cup (130g4½oz) icing (confectioners') sugar

1 tablespoon cream

METHOD

Preheat the oven to 180°C (350°F). Grease and flour a large fluted kugelhoph or deep ring pan. Arrange the oven shelf in the bottom third of the oven.

Combine all the flours, baking powder and salt in a bowl and, using a little balloon whisk, combine together. Set aside. (I am a lazy cook and NOT a fan of sifting, this little cheating method works well).

Place the sugar, eggs and vanilla into the mixing bowl on your standmixer. Turn to medium high speed (speed 8) and beat with the beater attachment for at least 5 minutes until very thick and creamy. This needs to be luscious and thick, the mixture will fall back on itself and hold its shape.

Reduce the speed to low (speed 1). Add the flour, milk, yoghurt and the butter. Beat on medium high speed (speed 6) for 1 minute or until thick and smooth.

Spoon and blob half of the mixture into the pan. Add the cocoa to the remaining mixture and mix on low speed (speed 1) for 10 seconds or until combined. Spoon and blob the cocoa mixture onto of the vanilla mixture. Smooth over the top (don't leave any peakie bits).

Bake 50 minutes until firm and golden. Very lightly touch the surface with your fingertip: it will feel just firm. If the centre feels a little moist, cover with a sheet of foil, securing to the sides, and cook covered for 5 minutes if it needs extra cooking.

Stand 10 minutes before removing from pan. Carefully place the cake on a cooling rack and cool completely. Place a dinner plate underneath the rack and drizzle the caramel icing over the cake. Allow to set before serving.

CARAMEL ICING

Place the sugar, butter and cream into small heavy-based saucepan. Cook stirring with a wooden spoon over a low heat until mixture bubbles lightly and is smooth and glossy. Stir in the icing sugar. If a thinner consistency is wanted, stir in the extra cream.

Drizzle over the cake allowing the icing to roll down the sides of the cake.

What went wrong

- Incorrect measuring (particularly too little butter, sugar or too much milk).
- Incorrect oven temperature? Too low cake will be pale and dense; too high cake will cook unevenly be hard on the outside edge and not cooked in the centre.
- Underbeating the eggs and sugar—this will produce a denser heavy texture.
- Overmixing—this toughens the batter.
- Too-high shelf placement—the cake will dry and crack.

Delicious Banana Cake

Makes 1 large cake

EQUIPMENT

22cm (8½oz) cake pan, standmixer, mixing bowl, small balloon whisk, cake rack

. . . .

INGREDIENTS

2 cups (270g/9½oz) self-raising (self-rising) flour (or gluten-free flour, see gluten-free section in the Introduction)

½ teaspoon bicarb of soda

pinch salt

3 large over-ripe bananas, roughly broken into pieces

125g (4oz) unsalted butter, softened to room temperature

¾ cup (165g/5½oz) brown sugar (lightly packed not pressed into the cup)

¾ cup (150g/5oz) caster (superfine) sugar

2 teaspoons vanilla extract

3 large eggs, room temperature

½ cup natural yoghurt mixed with 1 teaspoon vinegar

This is my twist on a truly delicious cake by the lovely food writer Belinda Jeffrey. I hope one day she tries my version!

METHOD

Preheat the oven to 180°C (350°F). Butter and line the base and sides of a deep 22cm (8½oz) round cake pan. Place the oven shelf in the bottom third of the oven.

Combine the flour, soda and salt into a bowl and using a little balloon whisk, combine together. Set aside.

Place the banana chunks into the mixing bowl on your standmixer. Using the beater, beat on medium speed (speed 4) for about 20 seconds or until mashed. Remove and set aside. Wash and dry the bowl and beater.

Place the butter, sugars, vanilla and eggs into the mixing bowl. Using the beater beat on medium high speed (speed 8) for 7 minutes or until very thick and creamy

Add the banana, flour mixture and yoghurt. Mix on low speed (2) until just combined. Increase to medium low (speed 4) and beat 1 minute or until creamy.

Pour the batter into the pan. Spread the top down with a spatula until the top is smooth—no peakie bits.

Bake 45–50 minutes. Or until the cake is golden and firm to touch. Stand 5 minutes before removing from the pan. Place on a cooling rack to cool completely.

Spread with Cream Cheese Frosting (see recipe).

What went wrong

- Not weighing ingredients properly. The ratio of dry ingredients to butter and eggs is important.
- Use only ripe bananas. Firm bananas will not mash, flavour will be unpronounced and the texture uneven.
- Butter must be at room temperature (very soft) so it beats in with the bananas.
- Too much sugar—cake will be crusty on top with sugar speckles and can have dark spots.
- Too much beating once the flour is added (the cake can puff up then sink, and the cake will toughen if over-beaten).
- Incorrectly sized cake pans (too large cake will be flat have low volume and overcooked; too small the batter will overflow and the centre will be doughy.

Nutty Carrot Cake

Makes 1 large cake

EQUIPMENT

*scales, measuring cups and spoons, peeler, grater,
standmixer, spatula, 22cm (8½in) cake pan, aluminium
foil, cooking rack*

. . . .

INGREDIENTS

3 medium carrots

3 large organic eggs, room temperature

½ cup (120g) caster (superfine) sugar

⅓ cup (80g/2½oz) lightly packed brown sugar

1 teaspoon vanilla extract

250ml (9fl oz) sunflower oil (or a vegetable oil)

1 cup (200g/7oz) pitted dried dates, roughly chopped

¾ cup (70g/2½oz) shredded coconut

½ cup (50g/1¾oz) walnuts, very roughly chopped

½ cup (75g/2½oz) dried apricots, roughly chopped

*½ cup (100g/3½oz) fresh pineapple, chopped (or canned in
juice, lightly drained)*

*2¼ cups (340g/12oz) self-raising (self-rising) flour (or gluten-
free flour, see gluten-free section in the Introduction)*

½ teaspoon each ground cinnamon and mixed spice

*extra 1 cup (150g/5oz) pistachio nuts or walnuts, lightly
toasted for decoration*

*A classic cake, this is my spin full of
lovely bits and pieces—and don't forget
the cream cheese frosting.*

METHOD

Grease and line the base and sides of a deep 22cm (8½in) cake pan. Preheat the oven to 170°C (340°F).

Peel and coarsely grate the carrots, set aside.

Place the eggs, sugars, vanilla and oil into the bowl of a standmixer. Using the beater attachment, beat 1 minute on medium speed (speed 6) or until thick and creamy.

Add the dates, coconut, walnuts, apricots, pineapple, and orange rind. Mix 10 seconds on low speed (speed 2).

Add the carrots, flour and spices and mix on low speed (speed 2), for 30 seconds or until well combined. Don't overmix.

Pour into the prepared pan and smooth over the top. Bake on lower third of the oven for 30–40 minutes or until just firm. Cover the top with a sheet of greased foil (be sure to grease it or it will stick to the cake) securing it to the sides of the pan. Bake a further 10–15 minutes or until the cake if firm to touch. This covering ensures the cake steams through evenly in the centre.

Allow to cool 10 minutes before removing from the pan and placing on a cooling rack. Cool completely before frosting. If the cake isn't completely cool the icing will just slip off!. See Cream Cheese Frosting for recipe.

Decorate with the pistachios or walnuts once frosted.

What went wrong

- Not weighing ingredients properly (ratios, ratios, ratios—they should be just right!).
- Too much sugar—cake will be crusty on top and may have speckles or look too brown.
- Too much beating (cake will be tough and may end up with a crack in the centre).
- Incorrectly sized pan—if too big cake will overcook and be flat, if too small it will overflow and bloom.
- Frosting—too much butter or too much sugar will result in the wrong consistency. Overbeating will cause the icing to become thin and it will slip off and lumps in the icing sugar must be sifted out before mixing.

All-in-one Scones

Makes 7

EQUIPMENT

scales or measuring cups and measuring spoons, standmixer or mixing bowl, hand whisk, knife—optional, round cake pan or baking tray, scone cutter

. . . .

INGREDIENTS

270g (9½oz) plain (all-purpose) flour
1 tablespoon baking powder
2 tablespoons pure icing (confectioners') sugar
½ teaspoon salt
150ml (5fl oz) thickened cream
150ml (5fl oz) soda water
75g (2½oz) extra flour for dusting

Recipe can be doubled or tripled if desired!

If you find scones too challenging or you constantly make doughy, heavy scones, try this method—using cream, mixed in a standmixer and cooked in a cake pan.

What went wrong

- Incorrect oven temperature—too hot will burn the top before they are cooked through, too cool and scones won't brown and rise.
- Overmixing with heavy 'hands' causing scones to be dense and flat.
- Too much baking powder—this will give the scones a metallic aftertaste.
- Too sweet, using lemonade instead of soda water.
- Dry and heavy looking.

METHOD

Weigh and measure all ingredients correctly

Preheat oven to 200°C (400°F) fan-forced, 220°C (430°F) in a conventional oven.

Lightly grease a 22cm (8½in) heavy-based cake pan.

Place the flour, sugar and salt into a mixing bowl on the standmixer. Attach the flat beater. Turn to low (speed 1) and mix for 2 minutes until well combined.

Combine the cream and soda water together in a jug and whisk to combine. Add the cream mixture in one go and mix for 10 seconds or until mixture forms a STICKY dough.

Flour hands and bench well. Tip out sticky mixture and lightly knead by lifting the dough up and over two to three times until a soft ball forms.

Lightly pat out to about 3cm (1¼in) thick. Flour a medium-sized scone cutter and press out a scone. Place into the cake pan, placing the scone against the side of the pan (this will help the scone cook with a straight side). Continue until the dough has been used.

Wipe your finger around the inside of the cream bottle or measuring cup and spread a touch of cream lightly over each scone. Bake on the centre shelf for about 12 minutes. Cool for 2 minutes, remove to a cooling rack and wrap in a clean tea towel until serving.

Tip: I find many cream (and lemonade) scones simply too sweet. This is my complete success version, using those important bubbles. Cream is another easy ingredient and making scones is a prefect way to use up that cream that's no longer at its freshest.

Fluffy Pancakes

EQUIPMENT

scales or measuring cups and measuring spoons, standmixer with flat beater attachment or blender, large pouring jug or large ladle, good heavy-based frying pan, pastry brush, egg slide

INGREDIENTS

2 cups (270g) self-raising (self-rising) flour (or gluten-free flour, see gluten-free section in the Introduction)

1½ teaspoons baking powder (add th is little extra just gives a better lightness)

⅓ cup (80g/2½oz) caster (superfine) sugar

2 large eggs

400ml (14fl oz) buttermilk (or use milk with 2 teaspoons white vinegar, but the buttermilk gives the best result)

70g (2½oz) butter, melted and cooled

METHOD

Measure and weigh the ingredients properly.

Combine the flour, baking powder and sugar in a mixing bowl, combine with a small balloon whisk.

Place into a mixing bowl on a standmixer. Add the eggs, buttermilk and half of the cooled butter. Beat with the beater attachment on medium speed until smooth.

Pour the mixture into a jug (this makes for easy pouring). Heat a frying pan over a medium heat (not too hot or it will burn).

Brush the frying pan with a little of the remaining butter. When hot and a little bubbly pour about ⅓ cup of the batter into the pan (depending on size of the pan you may be able to cook more than one at a time, usually two will fit). Cook for 2 minutes or until bubbles appear and the underneath is lightly golden. Flip over pancake gently and cook for about 1 minute on the other side.

Remove to a plate and keep warm covered with a sheet of foil. Repeat with the remaining butter and batter.

Serve with good maple syrup or your favourite jam.

What went wrong

- Not measuring ingredients correctly.
- Too much flour and too much mixing makes a dense, heavy, tough pancake.
- Not allowing room in the pan for pancakes to spread (yes you get one big one).
- Pan too hot making the pancakes overcooked on the outside and gooey in the centre.

Pikelets

Makes 14

EQUIPMENT

scales and or measuring cups and spoons, liquid measure, standmixer and beater, heavy-based frying pan, large jug or glass bowl, ladle (optional), egg slide or spatula, dinner plate

. . . .

INGREDIENTS

1¼ cups (175g/6oz) self-raising (self-rising) flour (or gluten-free flour, see gluten-free section in the Introduction)

2 tablespoons (40g) caster (superfine) sugar

1 egg, room temperature

200ml (7fl oz) milk, room temperature

2 teaspoons white vinegar

100g (3½oz) butter, melted and cooled

extra butter for cooking (if required)

Recipe can be doubled.

Lacy and light, tender pikelets, delicious with a good cup of tea.

METHOD

Place the flour, sugar, egg, milk, vinegar and half the butter into the mixing bowl on your standmixer. Using the flat beater attachment mix on low speed (2) for 30 seconds or until a smooth batter is formed. Remove to a large jug or glass bowl. Refrigerate 10 minutes (this really does make a difference to the texture of the pikelet, so if time allows, please rest the batter).

Heat a large, heavy-based non-stick frying pan over a medium heat. Add about 2 teaspoon of the remaining butter and swirl it over the pan.

When the butter is a little foamy, add about 2 tablespoons batter using a tablespoon measure or a small ladle. Add the batter slowly so the shape of the pikelet is smooth and even. Add two to three more pikelets to the pan.

Cook over a low heat for about 1 minute or until some small bubbles appear on the surface (and the underside will look golden and lacy).

Flip over carefully (with a spatula or egg flip) and cook 15 seconds or until just firm. Remove from the pan (carefully with the egg slide or spatula) and place on the a plate.

Repeat with the remaining butter and batter.

Tip: Standing the batter relaxes the mixture, which produces a softer pikelet. Best eaten on the day of cooking.

What went wrong

- Incorrect measuring (particularly too much milk or too much flour), this makes the batter too thick or too thin!
- Overmixing—the batter becomes tough and leathery.
- A too-hot pan and the butter burns meaning the pikelet will overcook on the outside and be raw in the middle.
- Not measuring the batter (you'll end up with big and small pikelets)!

Rocky Road

Makes 1 large log

EQUIPMENT

scales, baking sheet or tray, chopping board, sharp knife, scissors, large saucepan with a heatproof bowl to fit into the top, spatula or wooden spoon, baking paper, loaf pan

. . . .

INGREDIENTS

100g (3½oz) hazelnuts or pecans

400g (14oz) good-quality dark eating chocolate

50g (1¾oz) unsalted butter

20g (²/₃oz) copha (vegetable shortening)

2 teaspoons vanilla extract

100g (3½oz) white marshmallows (cut in half—use scissors)

50g (1¾oz) good-quality wine gums or your favourite jubes (cut in half—use scissors)

A little square of this will bring a smile to anyone's face.

METHOD

Preheat the oven to 180°C (350°F). Place a large sheet of baking paper into the loaf pan allowing it to overlap the sides—these sides will act as handles when removing the set mixture.

Place the nuts on the baking sheet. Toast 7 minutes or until lightly golden. Remove from the tray and roughly chop.

Half-fill the saucepan with water. Place a heatproof bowl into the pan, making sure it fits well and the bottom of the bowl does not touch the water. Place the chocolate, butter, copha and vanilla into the bowl (make sure the bowl is dry, there must be no water because the chocolate must not get wet).

Place the saucepan over a medium-low heat and heat. Allow the chocolate to slowly melt (don't stir too much or play with the chocolate).

As the chocolate begins to melt, check the heat is not too high (too much steam escaping from the saucepan can make the chocolate seize and become unusable). Once melted carefully remove the bowl from the hot water.

Stir for 1 minute with a clean dry spatula until the chocolate mixture cools. Add the nuts, marshmallows and jubes. Gently fold through the melted chocolate.

Pour the mixture into the prepared pan, spread the mixture into the corners.

Refrigerate for 30 minutes or until set. Cut into pieces.

Store in a sealed container for up to one week.

Tip: The mixture can also be made in the microwave, but this needs patience. Repeat steps as above but place bowl (without the saucepan filled with water), into the microwave. Heat on medium-low heat for 1 minute intervals, stirring well in between. The microwave often seizes and burns chocolate—I prefer to use the saucepan method.

What went wrong

- The wrong type of chocolate (high sugar or high emulsifiers).
- Heat too high when melting, causing chocolate to become grainy and dull.
- Don't add the marshmallows when the chocolate is very hot as the marshmallows will melt and become gooey.

Extras

Real Chocolate Icing

Covers one large cake

EQUIPMENT

heatproof mixing bowl, small saucepan, small mixing bowl, small hand whisk, measuring cups, standmixer with beater attachment

INGREDIENTS

200g (7oz) good-quality chocolate (milk or dark), roughly chopped
300g (10½oz) unsalted or salt-reduced butter, at room temperature
200g (7oz) icing (confectioners') sugar mixture

METHOD

Choose a heatproof bowl that just sits on top of the small saucepan. Fill the saucepan with about 2 cups water. Place the chocolate into the heatproof bowl. Heat over a medium low heat and allow the chocolate to melt, stirring occasionally with a metal spoon. Always use a metal spoon when working with chocolate as a wooden spoon can hold water that can seize your chocolate—we don't want that.

Take care that the heat is not too high and that NO steam goes near the chocolate or it will seize.

Stir gently as the chocolate is melting (don't overmix or stir during the melting).

Remove the bowl from the heat and set aside to cool.

Beat the butter in the mixing bowl of a standmixer using the flat beater until nice and creamy. Place the icing sugar into the small mixing bowl and whisk with the hand whisk to remove any lumps.

Turn off the mixer, add the chocolate and beat on medium speed until fluffy. Mixture can be covered and set aside on the bench until needed. If refrigerated it will set too firm to spread on a cake.

What went wrong

- Not weighing ingredients properly. The ratio of butter to chocolate to icing sugar is very important.
- Melt the chocolate gently and keep any steam or water away from the chocolate (or it will seize).
- Overmixing (this will cause the chocolate to split and seize).
- The butter must be at a soft room temperature (chilled butter will be too cold to beat to a fluffy texture).
- No lumps in the icing sugar (or you'll have a lumpy icing).

Drippy Yoghurt Icing

Covers one large cake

EQUIPMENT
small mixing bowl, small whisk, rubber spatula

INGREDIENTS
½ cup (50g/1¾oz) pure icing (confectioners') sugar
¼ teaspoon ground cinnamon or cardamom (and a little extra for
  sprinkling)
2 teaspoons vanilla natural yoghurt

This recipe can be doubled or tripled.

METHOD
Place the icing sugar and ground spice in a small bowl and, using a small whisk, stir well to remove all lumps (I am a lazy cook and NOT a fan of sifting, this little cheating method works well).

   Add the yoghurt and stir well with a spatula until smooth.

Tips: Icing can be used to cover any cake (or cakes) that you like. I like to place the cake(s) on a rack with a plate underneath to catch the drips as they drizzle down the sides. Once iced, place into the fridge to set, then sprinkle with the spices before serving.
   This icing goes lovely with the Little Lemon Cakes (see recipe).

This delightful tangy icing drips down the side of your cake and looks amazing and it tastes just as good!

What went wrong

- Not weighing ingredients properly (the ratio of icing sugar to yoghurt is extremely important).
- LUMPS—no lumps in the icing (confectioners') sugar please!
- Pure icing (confectioners') sugar will give a slightly firmer icing that will set more firmly than if icing (confectioners') sugar mixture is used.

Cream Cheese Frosting

Makes enough to generously cover the top and sides of a cake.

EQUIPMENT

measuring scales, measuring cups and spoons, small mixing bowl, hand whisk, spatula, standmixer with beater attachment

INGREDIENTS

250g (9oz) pure icing (confectioners') sugar

500g (17½oz) cream cheese, softened at room temperature, roughly chopped

75g (2½oz) butter, room temperature

2 teaspoons vanilla extract (or the scraped centre of a nice plump fresh vanilla pod)

2 teaspoons finely grated lemon or orange rind (optional)

METHOD

Place the icing sugar in the small bowl and lightly whisk to remove the lumps (I am a lazy cook and NOT a fan of sifting, this little cheating method works well).

Place the sugar into the mixing bowl on the standmixer with the beater attachment. Add the cream cheese, butter, vanilla and grated rind (if using).

Turn to low speed (1) and mix 10 seconds to just combine. Increase the speed and beat on medium high (8) for 30 seconds or until light and smooth (don't overmix).

What went wrong

- Not weighing ingredients properly. The ratio of icing (confectioners') sugar to cream cheese is very important—too much icing sugar will actually make the frosting runny.
- Cream cheese and butter must be soft at room temperature, which means you can squeeze it easily between your fingers (chilled cream cheese or butter will be too cold to beat to a fluffy texture and will need to be overbeaten or create lumps).
- Don't overbeat—the cream cheese is high in moisture and overbeating causes it to thin out.
- No lumps (the lumps must be whisked out or sifted out of the icing sugar).
- Pure icing (confectioners') sugar will give a slightly firmer icing (but icing sugar mixture can still be used).

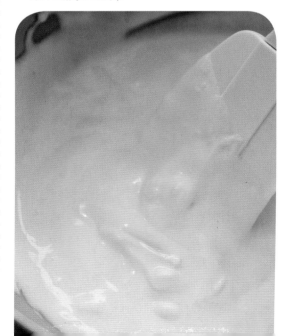

Milk Chocolate Mousse

Serves 6–8 (with loads of fresh berries)

EQUIPMENT

scales, liquid cup and spoon measures, small heavy-
based saucepan, stainless steel or heatproof bowl,
spatula, standmixer with mixing bowl, beater and whisk
attachments

. . . .

INGREDIENTS

250g (9oz) good-quality milk (or dark) chocolate, broken
into pieces (I like a couverture, good quality chocolate or a
good quality eating chocolate)
300ml (10½fl oz) thickened cream
2 tablespoons caster (superfine) sugar
4 large eggs, at room temperature (in the cooler months or if
the eggs are kept in the fridge, I pop the eggs into a bowl
of warm water to make sure they are not cold)
1 teaspoon vanilla extract

*Tip: You can replace milk chocolate with dark if you
like.*

METHOD

Half fill a small saucepan with hot water. Place a heatproof
bowl into the saucepan (this can be stainless steel or
heatproof glass) ensuring the bottom of the bowl does NOT
touch the water. The fit of the bowl is important, as no
steam must escape from the saucepan.

Place the chocolate into the bowl. Place over medium
heat and allow the chocolate to melt slowly, stirring
occasionally (be patient and don't overmix or overstir the
chocolate). Once the chocolate is melted, remove the bowl

What went wrong

- Overbeating once you've combined the mixture. This will take all the gorgeous air out of the mousse and turn it into chocolate soup!
- Overheating the chocolate or mixing it with any steam or water—the chocolate will seize and go lumpy.
- Overbeating the egg white (they will separate).
- Temperature: all ingredients must be at the same temperature! Make sure the egg mixture is NOT colder than the chocolate mixture or it will seize and be lumpy with pieces of hard chocolate throughout.

from the saucepan and set aside. Don't overheat the chocolate or allow any water or steam to touch it.

Place the cream into the mixing bowl of your standmixer. Using the whisk attachment, whip the cream on high speed (8) until soft peaks form. Remove from the mixer and set aside.

Separate the egg yolks and whites carefully. Make sure there is NO yolk in the white! (see technique on 'Separating eggs' page 23). Place the egg yolks and vanilla into the clean bowl on your standmixer. Using the beater attachment, beat on medium speed (4) for 2 minutes.

Pour in the warm chocolate and mix until just combined. (about 10 seconds). Remove this mixture to another bowl and set aside. Wash and dry the mixing bowl.

Place the egg whites into the clean and dry mixing bowl. Using the whisk attachment, whip the egg whites on high speed (10) to 'soft peaks' (don't overbeat).

Add in the sugar and continue whisking for 2 minutes (or until the mixture is a thick and glossy-looking meringue).

Turn off the standmixer and wipe down the sides with a spatula. Turn the mixer to low (speed 1) and pour in the chocolate mixture (adding it quickly). Continue whisking for 5 seconds or until just combined (don't overmix). Then add the whipped cream and whisk a little more, until just combined. (don't overmix).

Pour mousse into a serving dish. Dust top with cocoa and refrigerate for 3 hours or until firm (or even overnight if you prefer). Serve with loads of fresh berries.

INDEX

ACKNOWLEDGEMENTS

I have lots of gratitude and a long list of thanks to many of my industry greats.

A collection of amazingly skilled home economists and food consultants, who have shared and often steered me over a long 25-odd year road of recipes. At times we laughed (and cried) through many, many days of recipe testing, food photography shoots, prep days, filming days. All of these come together as the backbone of being a home economist, with the job of getting that recipe/technique/image or food show just right.

There are too far too many in the industry to acknowledge individually, but I must mention Lucy Kelly and Janet Lillie. I thank you both from the bottom of my heart.

Also, thanks to the iconic legends who do not know me, but who I feel I know. I have cooked, read and reread your recipes. Julia Child, Delia Smith, Margaret Fulton, Maureen Simpson, Joan Campbell, Stephanie Alexander, Nigella Lawson and Belinda Jeffery. A thank you for the hundreds and hundreds of hours of total immersion in food joy and sound culinary advice that you have shared.

A project like a book requires commitment and patience and words of advice from respected and experienced ones. There are many: Alana (and Dean and their beautiful view and kitchen, so kindly shared); my dearest gorgeous friend Di, as well as Janine for the washing up and a spot of shopping; Sunny and Janet for all those divine props, props and props, Marina and Belinda. Colleagues Sue Shepherd and Spencer Clements for your true friendship and invaluable professional advice. To all at Peter McInnes: thank you for your constant faith, trust and support, and allowing me to share and indulge in your beautiful, iconic products.

Thank you to my husband and family for allowing me to drive you nuts with the never-ending cooking, recipe testing while constantly taking over the family kitchen! A special mention to my darling daughter Lucy for those much-needed cups of tea and a smile right when I needed it.

A special mention must go to Simone 'Simi' Gordon who is always there with encouragement and wisdom. Thank you Linda Williams for believing and insisting and steering me through these uncharted waters.

Hugs and love to you all. I hope you like the result!

Thank you to Sally Lukey, my divine yet bossy, 'far too organised', bright and sparky assistant. You arrived from heaven I think! This project simply could not have been possible without you. Also, Liz Pleasants, thank you for lending a hand with some second testing.

To the wonderful Jack Sarafian, thank you for your commitment, encouragement, superb photography and friendship.

I simply could not have done this project without you all.

Jo Richardson

Published in 2014 by
New Holland Publishers
London • Sydney • Cape Town • Auckland
www.newhollandpublishers.com • www.newholland.com.au

The Chandlery Unit 114 50 Westminster Bridge Road London SE1 7QY United Kingdom
1/66 Gibbes Street Chatswood NSW 2067 Australia
Wembley Square First Floor Solan Road Gardens Cape Town 8001 South Africa
218 Lake Road Northcote Auckland New Zealand

First published in 2013.

A catalogue record of this book is available at the British Library and at the National Library of Australia

ISBN: 9781742573250

10 9 8 7 6 5 4 3 2

Managing director: Fiona Schultz
Publisher: Linda Williams
Project editor: Jodi De Vantier
Copyeditor: Bronwyn Phillips
Designer: Tracy Loughlin
Photography: Jack Sarafian
Food styling and food preparation: Jo Richardson
Food styling and food preparation assistant: Sally Lukey
Back cover illustration: Brooker Creative
Production director: Olga Dementiev
Printer: Toppan Leefung Printing Limited

Follow New Holland Publishers on
Facebook: www.facebook.com/NewHollandPublishers